WHAT PEOPLE ARE SAYING ABOUT
THE NEXT GREAT STEP

This book is a testament to Beth's understanding of how parents can best support their students to learn key life skills that will help them win that first job or internship, and make a difference throughout their career. *The Next Great Step* was the missing link to helping my son get the right job out of college. He just needed a little help tying it all together and understanding what employers were really looking for and how to communicate his value.

Steve Fleischer, Parent, Sales Leader - Healthcare & Benefits

The Next Great Step is a must-read that shares all the secrets for success that should be taught in college but aren't. Beth Hendler-Grunt shares a tried, tested, and true approach to conducting a successful employment search for new grads.

Harris Nydick, CFP, Co-Author, Common Financial Sense, and managing partner of CFS Investment Advisory Services

We are so pleased with how *The Next Great Step* approach helped our son land a job. This helped him to understand his strengths and allowed him to get focused on a specific functional area that fit his personality and career objectives. I am happy to let you know that he recently accepted a job as a sales representative for a logistics firm. We appreciate the impactful result that you were able to help him achieve. I will be sure to recommend it to friends and colleagues that have college kids and grads.

William D., Parent

Your college graduate is one of tens of thousands competing to enter the workforce. How can they stand out amongst the crowd? I highly recommend both parents and students read *The Next Great Step* to discover the secrets of landing an amazing job after college.

Nancy Josephs, Chief Executive Officer of Veritext

The Next Great Step helped my son understand what he wanted from a position and what he had to offer. He learned to articulate his strengths and assets in a convincing, confident, and clear manner. Within a matter of weeks of us utilizing Beth's approach, he was able to secure a great job and successfully interview for others. He learned how to present and differentiate himself from the rest of the pack.

Marlene L., Parent

I have collaborated on projects with Beth Hendler-Grunt and she is a passionate expert who will help college graduates land the job of their dreams. The Next Great Step book unlocks the key that will help parents successfully guide their grad to career success.

Joe Battista, Author of The Power of Pragmatic Passion: 7 Common Sense Principles for Achieving Personal and Professional Success, Hall of Fame hockey coach

THE
NEXT
GREAT
STEP

THE
NEXT
GREAT
STEP

THE PARENTS' GUIDE TO LAUNCHING
YOUR NEW GRAD INTO A CAREER

BETH HENDLER-GRUNT

THE NEXT GREAT STEP

THE PARENTS' GUIDE TO LAUNCHING YOUR NEW GRAD INTO A CAREER

BETH HENDLER-GRUNT

Published and distributed by Merack Publishing.

Library of Congress Control Number: 2022905689
Hendler-Grunt, Beth,
The Next Great Step

ISBN Paperback 978-1-957048-13-0
ISBN Hardcover 978-1-957048-15-4
ISBN eBook 978-1-957048-14-7

DEDICATION

This book is dedicated to the parents and caregivers who want to help their young adult achieve career success, but are not sure how. This is for you.

Some names and identifying details have been changed throughout the book to protect client privacy.

CONTENTS

FOREWORD

I met Beth Hendler-Grunt about five years ago thanks to my SiriusXM radio show *Dr. Dawn on Careers*. Because we welcome expert insights on our episodes, Beth became a frequent guest. Right from the beginning, there was something special about her "Next Great Step" approach and it stood out to me and to all our listeners. Though the job search for new college graduates is a difficult and often opaque process, Beth helped my listeners—and her clients—navigate it with confidence and she became my go-to person when addressing the unique challenges this population of job seekers faces.

Simply put, Beth *gets it*. She is deeply familiar with the hiring process as it is conducted today—not ten or twenty years ago. Beth knows how the process works and understands the common mistakes new grads and well-intentioned parents are making through no fault of their own. She's not just giving general career advice in these pages—she has a targeted approach that works for a specific population: students and new college graduates. She speaks directly to the missing link between where students are and where they need to be, thereby instantly reducing frustration and fear.

The truth is most career centers are profoundly under-resourced, especially in today's highly competitive and ever-changing market. It's not uncommon, unfortunately, for a career center to be crammed into the basement of a lecture hall or somewhere in a mostly forgotten dark corner of campus. Despite their importance, job search skills are not taught as part of the curriculum at most universities. This is changing slowly as people are starting to recognize that a university education is only getting more expensive—and the anticipated outcome of a graduate securing a job is not guaranteed. For decades, career services have been an afterthought for students, parents, and even university administration, but now people increasingly demand more from the money they are spending. And while I feel hopeful that over time career exploration will be a standard part of the curriculum, right now many students don't use the services that do exist. Even the students who find the time to stop into these offices often aren't sure how to use them or *when* to use them.

That's why this book is so necessary. It fills in the gaps felt by so many students and their parents. Beth is knowledgeable, compassionate, and extremely organized when it comes to sharing her expertise and in helping parents guide their new graduates with their job searches. She knows her stuff and walks her talk. As an expert coach, Beth not only understands how careers are built, she understands how to put all the pieces of that first full-time job search together in a way that is both intuitive and easy to execute. The process you'll find on these pages is meticulously thorough because Beth thinks about every piece of the puzzle. She is a great strategic planner who offers readers a powerful framework for succeeding in a way that is unique to their specific skills and interests. We've known each other for several years now and I've seen her impressive results firsthand.

The steps that Beth provides in this book are critical for the parents of young adults to understand and use, especially right now as we're seeing the job market changing so quickly and attractive industries becoming ever more competitive. What Beth teaches in these pages is something that students need to learn but won't automatically pick up along the way. When it comes to your child's job search, don't assume they know what they're doing. If they want to be competitive—and open up the best opportunities for themselves—new grads have to have a strategy.

In my opinion, this material should form the backbone of a required class in college, but for now, students only pick up these skills in bits and pieces and then struggle when looking to land their first real job. Many leave school believing all they need is a good resume, and while that is a part of it, in today's competitive landscape, the resume is actually only a minor tool in the overall job hunt.

Beth answers the question, "How do I stand out in this sea of tens of thousands of other applicants who also have a college degree and good grades and maybe also did an internship?" She teaches young people how to connect their experiences, skills, and aspirations with something a company or organization will see as valuable. Her expertise and background as a sales leader and business consultant make her uniquely able to bring new job seekers and employers together.

Beth connects the dots for this group in a unique way that I haven't seen before. She is a parent herself, so she understands what you are feeling. And interestingly, while this book is for a very defined audience—parents helping their new graduates with their first full-time job search—all the advice, exercises, and techniques she provides would be helpful to anybody in a career search. Anyone reading this book will get something out of it. The way Beth breaks down this daunting process into digestible steps is so palatable. Readers will be able to facilitate productive conversations using this book as a guide and ultimately help job seekers find satisfying full-time employment.

The best part is that by engaging with this book, job seekers will have the tools for navigating their careers in the years to come. When they understand how to assess their skills alongside the actual needs of today's job market, and build a story or pitch around this information, they stand out from the pack in a meaningful way. This is an ability that will serve your new college graduate throughout their careers.

It would be really hard to read this book, use what it teaches, and *not* be successful.

Dawn Graham, Ph.D.

Author of *Switchers: How Smart Professionals Change Careers and Seize Success*, TEDx Speaker, LinkedIn Learning Instructor, and former Director of Career Services at The Wharton School

HOW TO USE THIS BOOK

This book is designed as a guide.

It is full of practical applications and resources that will allow you to not only read through the concepts and ideas, but to take pen to paper and implement them for your own young adult.

As such, I've created downloadable templates that you can access AHEAD of diving into the content so that you can be prepared as you encounter them on the following pages. I'll remind you throughout the book when there's a resource.

Download these resources now.

nextgreatstep.com/bookresources

Please note that any advice referencing 3rd party software or social media is subject to change.

INTRODUCTION

Wasn't this supposed to be easy? Sending your child to college to get an education and expecting them to get a job upon graduating. What happened?

Young adults are graduating from colleges and universities unprepared for the job market. They are struggling to be proactive in their job search and meet the expectations of employers. Many can't communicate their value or speak about their skills in a way that connects with those who may hire them. Even when they are readily available, students are not utilizing the resources their colleges have to offer during their (at least) four-year journey—such as guidance from career services or relevant internship experience—to lay the foundation for a successful job search.

Some have no idea what they want to do, or they never felt particularly connected to their college major and don't know what kind of role would be a good fit. More importantly, many are not taught how to look for their first job. **This is a problem.**

The result is stress on the entire household, and tension between discouraged graduates and their frustrated parents. Though they may try to help, they find they cannot because they haven't conducted an entry-level job search in thirty years, don't know about the field their children are trying to enter, or are dismissed when they try to share useful pieces of advice. A new graduate living back home and stressed out about their lack of job prospects can impact the entire family dynamic. As the saying goes, "Parents are only as happy as their unhappiest child."

Parents call me because they realize it's time for an outside perspective and some expert guidance. They likely hired an SAT tutor or college advisor once upon a time—someone to get their son or daughter *into* their college of choice. Now, they need someone to get them *out* and on to their next great step.

Does this sound a little too familiar?

The data supports these feelings. 87% of college graduates believe they are ready to work but only 50% of hiring managers agree. 43% of this cohort will be underemployed after graduating.[1] Internships can help tip these stats in a new grad's favor—and it's helpful to note that one out of

---

1   D'Orio, Wayne, "Are Grads Ready to Work?" Human Resource Executive, April 11, 2018 Are Grads Ready to Work? | HRExecutive.com

ten internships takes place in the year *following* graduation. At least 60% of students in each graduating class since 2013 participated in an internship and/or co-op during their time in college and approximately 70% of employers offer their interns full-time jobs. Students who completed an internship are 15% less likely to be unemployed in the first years after college.[2] Yet a study recently completed using data from labor-market analytics firm Burning Glass Technologies, found that hiring for entry-level college graduate positions has recently fallen 45%, more than for any other category of education.[3]

As the parent of a new graduate, you read statistics like these and feel a stab of fear: the numbers hit close to home. You've done everything right and supported your young adult in every possible way for the past twenty or more years, but now you feel powerless as that elusive first (or right) full-time job offer fails to appear for your child.

As you and your family search for a way to fill in the gaps, I want to assure you the right job opportunity is out there for your child—a role in which they will continue to learn and grow. By helping them build the confidence and self-knowledge necessary not only to thrive in their first professional role, but

2   Milenkovic, Milica, "To Intern or Not to Intern: 30+ Eye-Opening Internship Statistics," Small Biz Genius: 30+ Eye-Opening Internship Statistics: 2021 Data And Trends (smallbizgenius.net) Accessed November 8, 2021.

3   Selingo, Jeffrey and Sigelman, Matt, "The Crisis of Unemployed College Graduates," The Wall Street Journal, Feb. 4, 2021; https://www.wsj.com/articles/the-crisis-of-unemployed-college-graduates-11612454124 Accessed June 24, 2021.

THE NEXT GREAT STEP

in their entire career, you equip them with skills that will serve your new graduate for decades to come.

This book is for parents who want to see their children achieve success, specifically a first real job offer or internship in their field of choice. It's for parents who are seeing that when it comes to their new graduate's job search, things are simply not clicking. This book is the answer for how to guide your child toward a career, especially when they are waiting, hoping, and randomly applying.

A New Approach

I've seen this problem play out for many years. My friends would say, "I don't get it. My kids went to a great school, earned a great GPA, and they can't get a job." At the same time, I was a corporate consultant noticing that my executive clients would pass over recent grads while positions in their companies went unfilled, and then express frustration about the lack of applicants. By explanation, they would claim young candidates "didn't get it" and that they did not want to invest in the time to train them.

I saw a big disconnect between employer expectations for hiring and the skill set recent grads thought they had for the workplace. *"What if students knew how to approach the job search like a CEO?" I asked. How could we create a solution to this ongoing problem?*

What if we taught college grads to have a strategy for their job search? And taught them how to differentiate themselves?

And finally, what if we taught them how to execute, and have a clear plan every time they meet a prospective employer? We tested these ideas with students and grads from community colleges to Ivy League schools, students with tremendous potential who lacked the skills we were teaching. Very quickly, the consensus was, "We need this. We need this type of help."

We learned that our concepts were new and fresh to these students, as they were not being taught these necessary job seeking skills in college. As one young man put it, he knows he has to climb the job search ladder but does not know how or where to start. We set the ladder up, with a strong foundation and an expert to guide them along the way.

Today, my team and I help new graduates think about the skills they have to offer in a way that makes sense to the organizations with whom they'll eventually work. We help your grad eliminate generalities in their communication and target specific roles and people in their network.

This book outlines our process for helping parents to empower their young adults to reduce fear, build confidence, and utilize proven strategies to land the job. Students and new college graduates assess where they are and where they'd like to go, but we have written this for you, their parents or guardians. Using the tools and processes in these pages, you'll be empowered to help your new grad define and communicate their core skills, target appropriate companies and specific people at those companies, come up with a meeting plan, and practice their interviewing techniques. This is a process your new graduate can begin with your help, with a trusted family friend, or with one of our certified coaches. Your child is three quarters of the way toward independent adulthood. I am here to help you help them on that journey by providing the Next Great Step.

In the first half, we'll explore some of the thoughts you as parents have shared about the hiring process as well as the misconceptions you may have about job-seeking—and why you are often unable to help your children get that first job offer. We will explain how new graduates *themselves* are feeling—and common mistakes they are making—in the midst of a process that might not be going as smoothly as they had planned. And we will share expert insight on how your new graduate is viewed through the eyes of employers as well as the disconnect between young job seekers' expectations and the reality of that first job. The second half of the book will share the solution to these problems with the tried-and-true proprietary Next Great Step process, as well as ways you can help your student succeed.

These life skills are not taught at most colleges or universities, among your student's or new grad's peer group, or even in the home. Yet these skills are worth hundreds of thousands, or even millions of dollars, throughout a career. The things we teach new grads are not just relevant for securing that first job but necessary for decades to come. Having the confidence to ask for promotions or raises, and look for new roles when the time is right, is invaluable. As a result of more fully realizing their professional potential, your grad's overall satisfaction and earnings will be exponential. If the average college tuition with room and board per year is $50,000,[4] and colleges can teach students skills that will enable them to get a job at $55k,[5] the return on investment of a college education over their career becomes a no-brainer. But when grads are unable to find work, flounder in jobs that do not require a college degree, or do not emerge with the skills needed to land a job their return on investment is not as high.

Our company has helped hundreds of grads land new jobs in all industries and fields, ranging from engineering and graphic design, to theater and digital marketing, and from accounting to positions at consulting firms and the top investment banks. We see the full range of majors and help graduates find positions in both the corporate and nonprofit worlds.

Not getting a job offer or a solid internship is such a disappointment to your student or new grad. They're all stunned when they reach what feels like an insurmountable roadblock. They don't know the game or how to present themselves.

It's time for a new approach.

---

4   "How Much Does College Cost?" CollegeData.com, https://www. collegedata.com/resources/pay-your-way/whats-the-price-tag-for-a-college-education Accessed November 8, 2021.

5   Hess, Abigail Johnson, "College Graduate Starting Salaries Are At An All-Time High," https://www.cnbc.com/2021/09/01/college-graduate-starting-salaries-are-at-an-all-time-high.html Accessed November 8, 2021.

KARA'S STORY

Michael was worried about his daughter Kara, who had graduated as a computer science major from a highly selective private university more than a year before we spoke. When she completed her coursework with a STEM focus and graduated with honors, everyone in the family thought Kara would have several job opportunities available to her. They believed companies would be competing to hire her, particularly as the family lived near many tech companies headquartered in a major city.

The reality of the situation turned out to be much different than anyone had anticipated. Kara's job search had been nothing but a struggle—an experience that deeply eroded her self-confidence and left Michael feeling desperate to help his daughter, yet he was not sure where to turn, or even what to say to her.

Today, she is feeling lost and disconnected. Over the past year, she applied to many jobs online, but when she did not see results, she got discouraged. She would send one email, but when the person she messaged did not follow up, Kara assumed they were not interested and did not reach out again. One setback led to another and another, and a year later, she's still living with her parents and feeling completely defeated.

It's difficult for any new graduate to stay motivated after going so many months without responses from any employers, and Kara has not been aggressive in pursuing opportunities. This is the first time in her young life she's failed so noticeably, and it feels as if the stakes could not be higher.

"The last person she wants to take advice from is a parent," Michael told me. "Even though I have corporate experience and have hired many candidates."

His feeling of powerlessness echoes that of many parents I've spoken to in the last five years. Kara's biggest challenge? Lack of confidence. She is so easily discouraged that she won't follow up with the people who could actually help her. She doesn't yet understand that the process she is trying to navigate is not about her. It is about how she can help a company achieve greater success because of her. Her job needs to be finding a job, but Kara is doing what countless new grads do when they don't get the results they're seeking: she has started coming up with excuses as to why she can put certain tasks off until tomorrow—which then becomes a week, a month, five months.

Kara and other new university graduates need structure, encouragement, accountability, and guidance. In most cases, parents can provide these things, but their efforts are often not well received.

Michael worries to the point where he cannot offer objective advice or a cool head. What is most important to him? For his daughter to feel good about herself and find a job where she is valued and making a contribution. He is much more concerned about these things than about her salary. He wants his daughter to have self-worth, to wake up every morning and feel a sense of purpose.

"I need someone to fill in the gaps," he concluded. "Kara is lost and I cannot help her."

THE PROBLEM

THE PARENTS' PERSPECTIVE

SECTION 1:
It's Not What They Promised

When your child got into the college of their dreams, you probably felt a weight off your shoulders: *We did it!* Adulthood, unlocked.

You got them to the finish line. Right?

In one sense, yes. But in another, not exactly. Getting into college and ultimately graduating is a huge—*huge*—accomplishment that you and everyone in your family should be proud of. Unfortunately, **one of the biggest misconceptions I hear from parents is the idea that their child's university will "take it from here" when it comes to securing them a job.** This is understandable as the admissions team and the school's overall branding and promotion may have focused strongly on post-graduation career outcomes.

I understand you and your student may have been sold a campus with an amazing career services center, or subscribed to the notion that your student can relax their freshman and sophomore years and worry about the job search later. While this sounds appealing, particularly after navigating the often highly pressurized admissions process, I'd like to gently burst this bubble. It might be wise for your son or daughter to think ahead to post-college life for the entirety of their college career—and be wary about leaving things in the hands of the campus career center (which may not be much help at all).

When you and your grad decided on which school they would attend, you assumed that they would receive solid career guidance at school. That the university would connect them with many potential employers and would have a solid internship or job.

Isn't that what they promised you on the campus tour?

Parents believe that career centers are more equipped and involved than they really are. Furthermore, according to a recent report, fewer than 20% of undergraduate students actually reach out to their school's career centers for advice on finding jobs or on finding and applying to graduate programs.[6] Another study revealed that only 17% of those

---

6   Fadulu, Lola "Why Aren't College Students Using Career Services?" https://www.theatlantic.com/education/archive/2018/01/why-arent-college-students-using-career-services/551051/ Accessed July 14, 2021.

who graduated from 2010 to 2016 said they found their college career centers to be "very helpful." Fewer than 40% said they found career centers to be "somewhat helpful," and 17% said the interactions were not helpful at all.[7]

Many colleges and universities do not devote enough resources to career services. A well-known large public university, for example, only had 16 advisors for *20,000 undergraduates*. That's one advisor for every 1250 students. Universities don't invest in career services the same way they might be willing to invest in a new stadium or a recreational activity center. Most universities feel their only job is to educate students, not to get them a job after graduation. **Life skills, such as networking, are not part of the curriculum.** Furthermore, the people in the career services positions that do exist have often been doing the job for thirty years. It may be hard for them to give relevant and personalized advice to students today, or for the student to relate to someone of that age. Universities, community colleges, and technical schools should be doing a much better job of lining up job shadowing opportunities and mentorships for their students with professionals in various fields and industries. There is a huge disconnect between what life is like as a student and what it becomes when a young adult starts working full-time.

Though career planning isn't part of the curriculum at most colleges and universities today, I think we're about to see a lot of

---

7   New, Jake, "Looking for Career Help" https://www.insidehighered.com/news/2016/12/13/only-17-percent-recent-graduates-say-career-centers-are-very-helpful Accessed July 14, 2021.

upheaval in higher education, particularly as families question the value of online/remote classes and the amount they're paying (or the amount their child may be borrowing) to cover tuition. Career services offices need a branding makeover or a major update on most campuses, because everyone needs a job after graduation.

One type of curriculum that I believe gets it right is undergraduate programs that include a mandatory internship in order to graduate. Colleges and universities with this type of requirement must foster and maintain deep connections with local businesses and organizations to ensure each student is placed in an internship. More universities need to follow this lead.

Avoiding Career Resources

Students also avoid school-sponsored career fairs because they may face rejection in these settings and that is uncomfortable. In addition, there are often hundreds of other students and long lines at these events. **They believe their peers have it all figured out and they're the only one who feels lost or overwhelmed.**

They think family or friends will link them to a job when they graduate, so attending a fair isn't necessary. In some cases, seniors will say, "I went to the career fair, but it was a waste of effort because the companies don't look appealing or they just told me to apply online." They come away feeling discouraged and unsure that their university can really assist.

Four out of ten students do not use career services or attend career fairs when they're at school. This is unfortunate, as **it is the only time in a young person's life when businesses are actively looking for them!** Furthermore, those who *do* choose to attend career fairs get practice meeting people and talking about themselves and their career interests. It's wise for students to attend career fairs and networking events in college even if they haven't yet declared a major as it's never too early to explore options, meet people, and get more comfortable asking questions about different job roles and industries.

Students are often not mature enough—or don't care enough early in their college journey—to pursue the resources that are available or attend the fairs created for them. Their thinking is, "I just want to enjoy going to school; I'll worry about that later." It's often a timing thing, "I'm just a freshman, why would I possibly need to go to the career fair?" Events like this seem very intimidating to new undergraduates, and many students feel as if they were just put through the wringer getting *into* college. So, when someone invites them to a career fair event, they'll say, "Who would I even meet there? I'm not ready and I have class that day." If the student is in the liberal arts school, they'll often say, "I don't know what my job's going to be yet, anyway." In addition, many of the companies that do work with a particular school's career services offices may be local, and that may not appeal to students who don't plan to stay in the region after graduation.

So many students do not have clarity on their major or course of study. I understand your child might be in this camp, but this doesn't completely excuse them from taking advantage of the career services resources or career fair events that exist at their school. Encourage them to think of it as an exploration. Those students who *do* go to career services or talk with advisors and local HR professionals are that much further ahead of those who are too shy or hesitant to do so. It's never too early. Guide your young adult (who may still be a college freshman or sophomore) to think of it like this: You may not be hungry now, but you know you'll need food soon so you better figure out where the dining hall is located and go see what they have.

Internships Can Wait... Or Can They?

In 2005, a young mechanical engineering graduate found an internship for a small theme park ride development firm. He pursued the opportunity, and in 2021 became the company's Chief Development Officer. Internships are important for several key reasons, and even if your son or daughter is only a college freshman, it isn't too early for them to think about one. A recent study showed that employers are more likely to respond to intern applicants who have had a previous internship, so that first experience matters more than you might expect down the road.[8] Internships help students gain firsthand experience and insight into how the working

---

8   David A. Jaeger, John M. Nunley, Alan Seals & Eric J. Wilbrandt, "The Demand for Interns" (National Bureau of Economic Research, February 2020) The Demand for Interns | NBER Accessed November 8, 2021.

world operates. They also help students and new grads see things through an employer's eyes—an attractive quality in a job seeker at any level. Employers say they prefer work or internship experience over a high GPA, in fact.

Students who anticipate what an employer is focused on will better relate to them and have greater success during their eventual full-time job search. Students should be able to answer the question, "What does a CEO/Department Head/Manager worry about?" There are many metrics that companies of all sizes track, including quarterly profits, number of units produced or services provided, time to market, customer service, etc. Students that demonstrate their understanding of what is important to an employer and then show how they can make the business more successful will ultimately see more job offers at the beginning of their careers than those who cannot do so.

Internships also increase students' networks of professional contacts. Students often have sizable networks that include fellow students, professors, parents and alumni. Internships add another layer of potential contacts and friendships to this list. The students who network and form relationships with their diverse connections can eventually use these relationships to help find new opportunities. This is a much more effective approach for a job search than applying online and crossing your fingers. It's never too early for your student to seek out and apply for internships in their field of interest—even as a freshman. Where an internship ultimately teaches them what they *don't* want to do, that knowledge is also invaluable, especially when it's built on experience.

It's time to expand our collective definition of internships. Instead of just thinking about some formal ten-week program at a large corporate consultancy, guide your student to do things like:

- Work a few hours per week at a local law firm, accountant's office, or veterinary clinic

- Offer to help a local small business plan an event, write content, or increase its presence on social media

- Serve as quality-control or a user experience tester for an e-commerce site

- Create a crowdfunding campaign for a local nonprofit initiative

- Design print marketing materials or a website for a student organization

- Offer to organize online file systems and delete or properly re-categorize unused data

- Do lead generation research and create a database of fresh contacts for a local entrepreneur or real estate agent

SECTION 2:
"I Thought I Could Help"

Something I often hear from parents whose children are having difficulty securing that first job offer is an issue we already touched on where I often hear, **"My daughter/son won't take my advice."** A huge misconception on the part of parents is that their advice will make that first offer for their children a piece of cake.

If you've ever thought, "I can make an introduction and my kid will get a job," then this chapter is for you. Of course, it's okay for parents to make introductions. However, your young adult may not be ready for them. I have heard many stories from parents who make introductions to the head of a company or department, and find that their child does not do well in the informational interview. They are too casual or assume Mom or Dad will ensure they get the job—which often does not happen. Be sure about your timing and understand what your new graduate's capabilities are.

Keep in mind that you and your child are not a team. **You are not both looking for your first job.** Yes, if you have interviewing or hiring experience, industry related experience, or specific company knowledge, it is perfectly fine to teach your child what you know about the process. Giving guidance on who to connect with and office etiquette tips are great. But don't take over—**finding a job is their**

job, not yours. Think about how you would mentor a friend's child.

My guess is you're butting heads and your son or daughter isn't listening to your words of wisdom. The problems may have their roots in decisions made years ago. For example, you may have nudged your child into a particular major, only to hear now that they want nothing to do with that field. Or, you may feel confused about the path they've chosen because it's different from your own and your child is shutting you out. I've had parents who are physicians that tell me, "My son is an environmental science major who studies sustainability. I am a well-educated person, but I don't know that field. I don't understand it and I don't know how to make connections for him."

As a parent, you want to see your children achieve success. When it comes to the job search, even though you've encouraged certain actions or techniques, things are not clicking. Your kid is not listening to you, they're waiting to get started, and everyone is frustrated. When parents call me in September after a long summer watching their child fail to line up a job offer, I often hear, **"I wish I knew then what I know now. I wish I understood how competitive the process is and that they should have started testing out the waters sooner.** Now the search is sputtering out and they're not networking at all."

It's hard to know the right thing to do. You've put a lot of faith into your son or daughter's school to help, you've tapped out your own connections, and you might be thinking it's just a numbers game—*something* will materialize if your child applies to enough positions, right? It's not your fault they're floundering. The truth is, however, that approaching a job search like a numbers game isn't particularly helpful. Submitting more resumes doesn't always generate more interviews, and more interviews do not always lead to more offers. It's about focus: quality over quantity.

Is It Too Late?

If you've picked up this book after your child has graduated, you may be feeling like it's too late to take action or that getting meaningful internships or entry-level job experiences won't be easy at this point.

That's not the case.

It's not too late and you are *not* behind. Yes, it's best for college students to begin planning for their futures early if they know what they want to do after graduation. But if your child hasn't done so, let me be the first to calm you: it's never too late for them to find their path.

Have they suffered a little bit? **Have they had enough pain in what they've done so far to reset?** Many new grads need a few months to realize that the vicious cycle of applying for random jobs online has gotten them nowhere. Going through that process often leaves them open to hearing how a successful job search is actually done. If your new graduate is curious about approaching things in a new way, this is the right time to get serious and begin a process that will lead to a job in their desired field.

It doesn't matter what time of year it is or how old the job seeker happens to be. **It matters how open and willing a person is: their readiness to listen and try new things.** When I hear, "I don't know what to do anymore," I know we can help.

It's never too late. Society creates a lot of pressure about timeframes: You've got to graduate in four years and have this job and get married and buy a house. I think we need to let go of the timing pressure that exists in our own heads. Everybody's on their own schedule and sometimes people don't figure out what they want until later in their career—or until after they've done a few things and realize what they don't like.

A first job is just that: a *first job*. It does not have to be forever, and it allows a young careerist to explore an opportunity that they hope to grow in. It's not uncommon to hear of "dream" jobs that ended up making people miserable. I was recently reminded of this by a good friend of mine at my college reunion. She accepted an incredible job at a sought-after investment banking firm and she *hated* the position. She pivoted quickly to medical school, and became a wonderful ICU doctor.

It's never too late.

What's The Tipping Point?

How long can you stand to watch your grad work on their job search without getting results? Or consider giving up completely because they've gotten so discouraged? The status quo isn't sustainable. Your child's job search has stalled and you're worried about their self-worth. You fear their lack of motivation could be a sign of something more serious like depression or anxiety. You see that your new grad is going through a very difficult situation and that it's changed them. In some cases, it may be their first major failure in life. They can look so discouraged, so stuck.

The longer the job search takes, the less capable a grad feels. They start to feel depressed over the continued rejection. It starts to alter their mind-set and shake their confidence. They avoid, procrastinate and start to give up.

If you hear yourself saying, "Just take any job," it might be time for you to step back as this is rarely the smartest move. When you notice yourself telling others, "My kid has no idea what to do. They don't feel connected to their major, and they really don't know what role to go into at all," it's time for them to gather more information. This means new graduates in this situation need to work on understanding what's out there—what kinds of jobs are realistically available and what they consist of.

Saying, "You can do anything!" creates problems as well. I recently spoke to a father whose son, Jason, went to a private university, studied sports management, and had great internships for a variety of pro teams. On paper, it made no sense that this young man had no job offers given such an impressive resume. His father, a lawyer, said, "I've tried to make some introductions, but something's missing. My son knows exactly what he wants to do, but can't close the deal." Graduates like Jason either can't get an interview, or when they do, they can't get an offer. Something's wrong.

In this case, the problem was a lack of interview preparation. Jason talked way too much and was way too general. He was all over the place in interviews, not focused. Even though he had done great things and his resume was actually getting picked up by the right people (which is half the battle), Jason was rambling on and on in person. I saw, after talking with him, that he was losing his interviewers. To his father, this young man was saying, "Oh, it's just very competitive." That wasn't the core problem as he had the credentials to compete—Jason had the required skills and experience. He just needed to stay focused and practice his interviewing skills. While we may deal with young adults whose confidence is flailing, sometimes they've been pumped up too much by you, their parents. I talked with a father not too long ago who is the CEO of a big company. He kept saying, "My son's a rock star. My son is the best; he's the most amazing!"

I said, "I understand that you love your son. But maybe the fact that you keep telling him this is hurting him." After he shared more about his son's career search, I offered my analysis:

His son sounded like he was a bit unfocused and that is why he was not getting hired.

This was a perfect example of overinflating a new graduate. I'm all about confidence but the situation was over the top.

SECTION 3:
The Mental Health Question

Mental health is an important topic today and one we cannot ignore as parents. **Job seekers often feel discouraged or even depressed due to the constant rejection they experience.** Some of it is concrete rejection: losing job opportunities to peers or other candidates, and some of it is perceived rejection: not hearing back after submitting dozens of applications. Discouragement also comes from thinking they are the only one who has not "launched" in their class or friend group.

Mental health issues are common in young adults. Therefore, if this is something you are concerned about, please know that you are not alone. One of my colleagues is Dr. Julia Turovsky, a clinical psychologist who specializes in anxiety and depression in young adults. The former director of the Anxiety Disorders Clinic at Rutgers University, Dr. Turovsky is an expert in the field and sometimes I refer families to her. She noted that rates of mental health diagnoses are unprecedented today—**upwards of 40% of the young adult population** reported experiencing anxiety or depression, according to the NIMH.9

I asked Dr. Turovsky for her insights and advice for parents when it comes to their young adults' mental health. She shared, "Each part of life brings a stretch and a challenge; organisms exist between periods of stasis and then periods of change. If there's too much stasis, we grow stagnant and if there's too much change, we become disorganized and chaotic. The general advice here is to understand that there needs to be these developmental shifts and that your child has to assume adulthood at some point. Helping them sometimes involves giving them a little room to struggle. Being uncomfortable, being stressed, and being worried are all normal and healthy emotions that challenge young people to develop further. These worries motivate and push them to develop further, to progress and feel confident in their decisions."

Anxiety and depression aren't always as easy to spot as we may think. "When a young adult hasn't been forthcoming about what's going on inside their head," Dr. Turovsky said, "these disorders can look like laziness, disorganization, lack of motivation, or apathy. But hiding behind those symptoms could be tremendous worry or perfectionism. Your child may feel like if they don't get the perfect job or the most prestigious

---

9   Vahratian A, Blumberg SJ, Terlizzi EP, Schiller JS. "Symptoms of Anxiety or Depressive Disorder and Use of Mental Health Care Among Adults During the COVID-19 Pandemic — United States," (MMWR Morb Mortal Wkly Rep 2021;70:490–494, August 2020–February 2021), http://dx.doi.org/10.15585/mmwr.mm7013e2.

job, they're a failure. Thus, holding back and not labeling the behaviors or the actions you're frustrated with is important—because all it does is take the young adult further into self-doubt, highlights their lack of competence, and impairs the relationship. Trying to assess *why* your child might be struggling and not jumping to a conclusion is wise. Of course, there are the kids who are fine and insist a job needs to be stimulating and interesting."

Parents need to be aware that when their kids can't get out of bed all day, they may be clinically depressed, not just lazy. "Depression can be easier to spot than anxiety because it has more physical and biological symptoms. The person looks really tired and sad. You can see changes in appetite, sleep, energy, focus, and concentration. Generalized anxiety, worry, perfectionism, obsessive compulsive disorder, or trauma can be much more difficult to see. People with anxiety are the highest functioning individuals of anyone with mental health issues. They look really good and they tend to be high performers or even overachievers."

While no one knows your child better than you do, we encourage involving a therapist, psychologist, or other mental health expert if you have concerns.

STEPHEN'S STORY

One of my very early clients, Stephen, was a brilliant kid who came out of the University of Michigan and eventually went on to UCLA. He was super smart. When he came to me, I asked, "Who has a vested interest in your success? Parents or mentors? What are their expectations?"

Stephen replied, "Both of my parents are PhDs. One's a PhD in civil engineering, and the other has a PhD in Biomedical Engineering. In their minds, you are only successful when you have a PhD."

The problem, of course, was Stephen didn't want to pursue a career in academia. He went to school to be a pharmacist and then realized he hated it but he thought might prefer being a nurse. Ultimately, Stephen decided he really enjoyed research. Today, he does cancer research in the lab at UCLA, but it was extremely difficult for him to break out from his parents' expectations and find a path forward that fit.

Creating Space and a Healthy Dialogue

As parents, we often communicate high expectations without even realizing it. We don't intend to make our kids stressed or feel guilty, but we do. **We have to remember to ease up on this unsaid pressure as they are trying to figure out their**

lives and we need to give them some emotional space to figure out what they really want.

"Criticizing and pointing out that they're struggling or expressing your frustration or doubt isn't helpful," noted Dr. Turovsky. "For example, saying things like, *You'll never get a job*, or, *What's wrong with you?* or, *You were lazy in college and you're lazy now.* are not useful." That said, the opposite isn't good, either. Some parents will tell their kids not to worry, that everything will work out and they will take care of it. Finding that gentle balance between being supportive and helpful and creating some independence is the key."

"Kids who just graduated college and are looking for jobs are really nervous about what they'll be able to accomplish in the world," she concluded. "Opening up and having a dialogue with your children is great—explore how they're feeling and support them and their emotions without intervening. Allow them to share and express some of their doubts and concerns without talking them out of those feelings or shutting them down. To get that conversation going, ask, 'How do you feel about finishing school?'"

"When young adults come to their parents with their problems or issues, they just want their parents to listen. They just want supportive validation, without the false platitudes. None of that generic stuff is as useful as saying, **'I hear you. I support you.** I know you're going to miss your friends. You're going to miss sleeping. I'm here to listen to your concerns.' **It's all about listening and validating, rather than problem solving or fixing."**

SECTION 4:
Things Have Changed Out There... Right?

A parent will say to their child, "Why don't you pick up the phone? Call some people!" To which the new grad says, "That's not how it's done anymore!"

Parents often don't realize how scared their kids are. That's why they don't want to "pick up the phone" to call a potential employer: "It's not our fault," a recent college graduate explained when I noted his generation's discomfort with calling people on the phone. He's right. Young people grew up texting or messaging on their devices; they've had much less practice than we did at age 22 talking to new people and looking them in the eye.

We as parents are unsure how to proceed because we looked for our first jobs so long ago. While some fundamentals in the process haven't changed, a lot of the steps are in fact different. Thirty years ago, you were looking in a newspaper for job openings and circling ads. You were also calling people on the phone and going to local networking events. Today, technology has altered the job search and many people are getting lost in the various platforms and social media channels.

New college graduates are seeing LinkedIn, Indeed, and all these boards where people post jobs and think, "This must be where you need to go." **They are over-relying on the technology and have become distracted and misguided about what it will actually do for them.**

Google and LinkedIn are phenomenal in terms of research, but using them doesn't lead directly to job offers even if candidates apply to hundreds of positions. Companies don't make buying or talent decisions; people do within the company. In the end, it's a person your new grad needs to communicate to...not a company or company image. *People hire people*, **not online resumes or tracking systems.**

Making a phone call, writing a good letter, showing you have a real connection, and explaining how you might be able to correlate your skills to the needs of a company has not changed. It's just that the technology in the middle has misled our graduates into believing that it alone can solve the problem. Parents think the same way, yet don't actually understand how any of it works. **If your child is one of 100 or 1,000 new grads who submitted a resume to a company that posted a job, the truth is they've done almost nothing.**

When you say, "Hey, you should probably call someone," that is great advice. It just seems so foreign to your child because no one else has ever said that to them before. It's easy for your new grad to say, "You don't know what it's like now." Or perhaps your child is willing to call but isn't sure what to say. Thus, they are afraid to actually pick up the phone.

Technology has its role to play, but there are a lot of misconceptions about what it can actually do for your student or new graduate. Part of our process is to put technology in its place—as a resource, not the answer. **There is a lot of bad advice out there for new graduates from friends and parents. As a parent, don't make this worse.**

The perfect example of this is a mom who tells her son, "Take a job in the field that I work in so I can make a connection for you." She's not interested in him finding a job or an internship that will ultimately be related to his career. The grad may learn some skills in that first role, but if they don't feel aligned to it or have the skills to be successful, they will end up leaving and starting the search all over again.

Often the only work experience some of our clients have had during and after college were jobs that don't traditionally require college degrees such as retail work, delivery driving, or food service. That's okay. There's something in every job your student has done that is useful. For example, working in a restaurant probably meant your child learned how to upsell drinks or dessert to customers. If they scooped ice cream, they learned customer service skills. If they worked as a delivery driver, they learned how to optimize their route. They are learning life skills: working on a team, showing up on time, and dealing with difficult customers.

Most new graduates just do not know how to sell these experiences and skills. A big piece of the Next Great Step approach is teaching students how to identify what they've learned and what they can do, and present themselves in the best possible light to employers.

"What's My Role Here?"

When parents call, they share many of the struggles and challenges they see their grad having. They pour their hearts out, saying, "I didn't even know your service existed until this morning. We just found you on Google and feel so relieved to be talking to someone who focuses on this problem." Often, their new graduate is not quite as on board to participate in our process as the parents are. Nevertheless, the overwhelming emotion we encounter with the parents at the beginning of a new client engagement is relief.

Parents can be very helpful if they know the right questions to ask and can actually help their children figure out their core skills. If you are able to, relax a little bit regarding what you think your child *should* be doing. If you as a parent can approach this process objectively, and try not to be emotional, *you can help*. Perhaps there is an uncle, a cousin, or a family friend who can facilitate this conversation using the framework you'll find in the chapters ahead. This can provide new grads with structure, as well as fuel for a fire that will energize their careers, not just in the months ahead, but for their whole lives. **Because understanding who you are, what skills you bring to the table, and how to effectively sell them is not just about landing that first job, it's about creating value over a lifetime.** This process lays a strong foundation they can build on—a foundation they'll use to eventually land that second job, that big promotion, and beyond.

Before we get to that, let's consider how your child is feeling about this process. By understanding their fears and mental blocks, you'll find it easier to support them on the road ahead.

CHAPTER ONE KEY TAKEAWAYS

- One of the biggest misconceptions I hear from parents is the idea that their child's university will "take it from here." Life skills such as networking are not part of the curriculum.

- You are not both looking for their first job. Finding a job is their job—not yours.

- Parents often wish they understood how competitive the process is and that they had seen their new grad begin the job hunt process sooner or had encouraged them to do so.

- When parents are living vicariously through their kids, the kids can sense it, and it makes them less likely to listen, take advice, or follow through on family connections.

- We have to remember to ease up on the subtle pressure we apply as new grads are trying to figure out their lives. They need a little space to figure out what they really want.

- People hire people, not online resumes. If your child is one of 100 or 1,000 new grads who submitted a resume to a company that posted a job, the truth is they've done almost nothing.

CHAPTER ONE RESOURCE

College students and their parents believe they have plenty of time when they're in school to make connections and gain skills. When senior year rolls around, new grads are thoroughly intimidated by the job search. We recommend the following career roadmap ideas which can be implemented regardless of the current stage of your child's journey.

Career Roadmap

Freshman

»   Get involved! Join clubs or participate in activities - at least one related to the major, one for fun.

»   Get to know your professors. Go to office hours or study sessions.

»   Create a resume. It's just a start—use experience from both high school and college.

»   Create a LinkedIn profile and start using LinkedIn to connect with classmates, professors and other contacts.

»   Visit your college career services to learn how they can support you. Focus on securing the summer internship.

For Sophomore, Junior, and Senior to-do's, please visit: nextgreatstep.com/bookresources

NEW GRAD'S PERSPECTIVE

SECTION 5:
"I Feel So Lost"

Students and new graduates are optimistic when they begin the job or internship search. They'll say things like, "Landing a job offer won't be that hard," or, "People say it's a great job market and I've been told I have a great resume. I'm going to submit it and hope to hear back."

A little bit of time passes, so they take a few additional actions: "I went to a few career fairs; my friend just got hired. I'll be fine." They might say, "Mom and Dad know someone who might be hiring; I'll talk to them next week." Then, the new grad waits for that one person to call back. They don't understand how to create a funnel of opportunities.

Nothing solid appears; they're waiting and living back at home.

More time goes by.

"No one is getting back to me," the new graduate says. A chill of defeat begins to appear and it curtails their energy and breeds self-doubt: "This job post looks interesting, but they want one to three years of experience. I'm not going to apply."

Nothing happens. The new graduate feels very alone and the situation feels extremely depressing to them. The cycle I often see starts with a graduate's attitude that everything is really great and it will be easy, then come the eventual setbacks and self-sabotage.

Finally, someone calls them back and they're so happy: *"This is it!"*

They land an interview, but they're so excited that they ramble when it begins, saying everything that comes to mind. They're often not prepared and the meeting gets away from them. No job offer appears.

It's an emotional roller coaster and it's very difficult to endure. As the parent watching them go through this, you don't know what to do. You just want to stop the ride and help them exit. You see your son or daughter get in their own head about why they aren't good enough. They're isolated and inertia sets in.

Your child ends up in a deep funk, and they start saying things that aren't even true, such as, "I'm the only one from my entire graduating class who didn't get an offer. Everyone else has a great job."

Or, "Why bother? I'll work retail or go to grad school." While these options may be viable for some, they don't address the issue.

What Should I Do with My Life?

Most young adults start their search by creating a resume or applying for jobs online. But that approach is skipping the most important step in the process. They need to answer the question, "What do you actually want to do?" This query brings out angst and stress because many young adults have *no idea* what they want to do. It doesn't matter that they had a specific major or part-time jobs throughout their college career. Grads are stuck—not only because they are overwhelmed with how to create the right resume, or network effectively, but because they have no idea what field or job they want to pursue. This makes the job search seem insurmountable at times.

I see it every day, students who chose their college majors driven by monetary aspirations, parental influence, and even pressure to be in "popular" industries (as deemed by their peers). They end up completely disconnected from their own interests, abilities, or real-world applications. They say things like, "I think actuarial science is where you make money and I have to make money, so that's where I'm going to go..." yet their skills or passions don't align with that field.

Or, "My mother and my father are lawyers so I guess I need to be a lawyer. I don't know if I really want that, but I'm doing poli sci."

Or, "My friends are doing engineering so I suppose I will, too."

Students and grads say, "I have to have this figured out and have a clearly mapped out plan because everyone else does." Or "I just wasted four years of school." It's okay. It's completely normal to not have it figured out. This feeling of being stuck can be overcome with a little patience, practice, and persistence.

Often grads and their parents will look for a personality assessment like the Myers Briggs test or the personal assessment tool like DiSC, to tell them what to pursue. By all means, if people want to use them, that's great. There are a lot of free online assessments out there as well.

People have been trained to believe that testing will help narrow their focus on what to pursue. It can give some helpful information but it's not a critical or defining step in your child's job search process. What we've found is that while these tests can give some insight, until a young adult learns firsthand what real people actually do for a living, no assessment can help them determine where they want to be. Instead, **clarity on their own skills in conjunction with informational interviewing and networking conversations help our young clients determine what they might want to move toward professionally.**

SERGE'S STORY

When new graduates start looking for that first job out of college, they struggle for several reasons. A big one is lack of good guidance from college advisors. This issue is reflected in the experiences of one of our most recent clients, Serge.

Serge is the US-born son of Romanian parents. Because he had to pay out-of-state tuition for all of his schooling himself, Serge was laser-focused on choosing a major at Purdue that would lead to a lucrative job offer post-graduation.

Like so many undergraduates, Serge pursued finance because of the perception of higher salaries in this field—his priority was to pay back his loans. Aspirational by nature, Serge is close with a cousin of his who works at a big hedge fund on Wall Street. This is an elite subset of finance that Serge envisioned for himself without really knowing that much about it.

Students are making huge life decisions without great advice or enough information. Serge had very little interest in finance and could not see how the classes he was taking connected to the real world. While in school, his grades suffered. He was actually brilliant but his GPA was very low due to boredom and him feeling annoyed. The lack of guidance from advisors was the key problem: they would tell him to take classes that had no relation to anything that he liked. No one at the university correlated the class content to what he'd ultimately want to do in the job market. Serge went to office hours only to see a long line of kids sitting out in the hallway, waiting to talk to a professor or get into a tutoring session.

"I couldn't fit in," he said. "They promised me there would be all the support, all this help and I'm not finding it." Worse, his GPA was too low for him to qualify for the investment banking program he'd been aiming for. Many of the top programs at the bigger universities demand at least a 3.5 GPA.

"Why am I paying so much and doing this by myself?" Serge would ask himself. As he neared graduation, he was directionless. He had put his faith in the college— that it would help him and hold his hand a bit. He'd had to take out many loans, which made him really mad. More than practically anything else, he wanted financial independence, yet he felt he'd dug himself into a hole. Upon graduation, with no job offers, Serge was angry and frustrated. He hadn't received the value he'd expected from his college education and his parents had no idea how to help him. Serge was feeling very cynical about everything.

It was actually his cousin, the successful Wall Street fund manager, who called me. He said, "I'm very concerned about my cousin. He doesn't know what to do and doesn't understand the steps of the job search. I'm not even sure if he's going to talk to you; he's so frustrated and upset with this process."

I let his cousin know that this is very common among graduates and that Serge's experience is something I see often. Sometimes it just helps to know you aren't alone in a situation like this! It's how you move forward from there that counts.

What Are the Controllables?

It doesn't matter if the job market is blazing or if it's terrible. Often, grads will see the media mention how the job market appears to be improving, yet they are not getting callbacks on their applications. New graduates need more direction when it comes to their job search no matter what's happening in the economy at large or with other factors they cannot control. I was recently asked, "What would you say to people if they're in a really tight job market or if we're going into a recession?" My answer is that things will be a lot more competitive but there will always be jobs. Job seekers will just have to really compete for them.

Even if there are a lot of jobs available in your field, your grad won't get one of them if they don't know how to create and manage new relationships. Ideally, they should be practicing this early on, as students. That's why attending career fairs before they declare a major as an undergraduate is helpful. Young adults often feel like everything has to be perfect before they approach new people or put themselves out there in a professional context, but that's not the case. Guide them to practice meeting new people and asking questions before they feel ready. That way, they aren't winging it later on.

Whether your student or new graduate finds themselves in an up or down market, the ability to adapt and form new connections—no matter the circumstances in the economy— is a crucial skill to cultivate. Unfortunately, new graduates are often anxious and overwhelmed. They don't know what they have to offer an employer and doubt their own qualifications. They're not sure what actions to take. Here is a small sampling of the sentiments we hear from this cohort:

"My biggest challenge is personal anxiety about the process. I am awkward in an interview."

"I'm not sure if I am doing the right thing or using the right process. Career Services has not been that helpful. No one is telling me if what I am doing is correct."

"I need deadlines to get stuff done. I don't know how to show confidence with employers."

"Yes, I've been reaching out to friends and colleagues in different careers to learn from them and networking with them but I don't know how to get to the next step."

"It's hard for me to tell which jobs are actually 'good' jobs just from a LinkedIn post. I want to find a career that fits me and I have been struggling with finding it."

More is Better?

We've worked with students and new grads who have applied to *hundreds* of jobs or internships online and never heard anything back. Either the posting was a scam, or the candidate didn't progress past the filters. They don't get anywhere with the "throw spaghetti at the wall and see what sticks" approach.

I ask new grads, "What are you applying to?" and they reply, "I'm applying to all these different random positions. I applied for a marketing job at Something Media, I applied to a technical writing job, and I applied to XYZ."

They think *more is better* when it comes to the number of jobs applied for, types of roles, companies, or industries. Often, there's not a real person on the other side of that "submit" button, no matter how many times your new graduate clicks it.

Sometimes, the opposite problem occurs. A new grad will say, "I have a really good opportunity, a family friend gave me an interview." They put all their eggs in one basket and then sit and wait because they think that this family connection will give them preferential treatment. This "overconfidence" may not only hinder their chances at the job, but limits their visibility into other legitimate opportunities.

Applying for 200 jobs is meaningless and putting all your eggs in one basket is equally unwise.

I encourage them to **focus on quality over quantity.** Does your child have a relationship with the person they'd like to work for? Have they connected or spoken with people that actually have the ability to hire them? Or get them to someone who does? Does that person understand your grad's skill set and the value that they could bring?

I Need a Better Resume, Right?

I hear this every day: "If you can just fix my resume so I can apply to more jobs, I'll be good."

Unfortunately, this is not all there is to it.

Finding a job or internship is a big (sometimes overwhelming) project, and we have found that many young job seekers don't know how to start or what to do. Many get too focused on small details—like their resumes—without keeping the big picture in mind. A perfect example is a student who reached out to us recently: "I am a recent graduate with a BS in Information Systems. Due to lack of experience, I am having trouble finding a job. I saw your services and was wondering if you could help me tweak my resume so I can reach out to more employers and jobs."

He thinks fixing his resume will enable him to reach out to more employers, but this thinking is incorrect. A perfect resume does not allow grads to reach out to more employers;

picking up the phone or sending an email does. **Fixing a resume does not fix anyone's job search.** It is just a small piece of the puzzle. Note this graduate's major—information systems graduates are in high demand. Nevertheless, this type of query is common as so many graduates are lost or completely paralyzed when it comes to the smallest details.

For over sixteen years, students have been following directions, turning in assignments, and relying on syllabi to determine what to do. Thus, many grads think that if I can just fix their resume, their LinkedIn profile, or their cover letter, that is all they need. Young people new to the job market are thinking of the job search as if it's just another course assignment. A good resume can certainly be helpful and should be designed with care, but that in itself is not sufficient. Similarly, I had someone tell me recently that his biggest challenge in the job search is his low GPA. Fair enough, but the low GPA is rarely the only reason a person is not getting work.

When we first developed and began testing the Next Great Step method, we didn't think about resumes or cover letters or LinkedIn profiles at all. Instead, we conceived of the program as a mini-MBA—a fast-track, real-life business approach to every part of securing a quality internship or job offer. Fixing resumes was never the focus of the work; instead of writing resumes, I cut my teeth learning to sell in the corporate world. Having hired a lot of people, I understand how hiring managers and business owners think.

We are teaching new graduates how to sell and *they* are the product. In addition to developing clarity and creating a targeted strategy, we teach struggling students and young job seekers concrete sales techniques like convincing somebody that they have a problem to be solved—and the candidate in front of them is the one to solve it. After our program, students and new grads walk into meetings with a clear purpose. **They help employers *want* to move forward with them by speaking intelligently about how they can solve that employer's problems.**

Which Jobs?

One of the problems with a new grad's first full-time job search is that there are so many different roles with different titles and different functions. It is very hard to know what a particular job even is when they are applying for it. Even someone like you or me, who may have been in business for twenty-five or thirty years, can get confused.

I usually have a good sense of what a role entails after doing a little digging, but students are not taught how titles work at different companies. A salesperson, for example, could be called an Account Executive, a Business Development Specialist, a Client Representative, or a Client Success Agent—and that's not an exhaustive list. There could be seven different phrasings for an entry level position. Newer grads don't understand this and are too quick to dismiss viable opportunities, saying, "Oh, that's not what I am looking for."

Even if a young person doesn't have any interest in insurance, it's possible they would like sales very much. A job could end up being much more interesting than its title might suggest. Students just don't know this, they are not taught it, and they don't know how to do the research to learn what a role may entail. This is unfortunate as it's not good to apply to a bunch of different jobs. **A company actually doesn't want a job seeker to be all over the place. They want that person to be really focused,** as in, "I know I want this kind of role and I can tell you exactly why I'm the right person for that job." Even if the job seeker may have some uncertainty about their focus, they need to convey their absolute specificity during that conversation or interview. Any ambiguity may convince a hiring manager that they are either not serious or not interested.

SECTION 6:
How Do I Network?

First time job seekers don't know what they don't know, and they are tired of hearing they "have to network."

We understand the sentiment.

"Throughout college, my professors, my advisors—*everyone*— said, '**You need to network with alumni,' but I don't get what that means,**" a graduate named Lena told me. "Does that mean having them as one of my connections on LinkedIn? Do I send them an email saying, 'Hi, I'm a student at the local technical college. Can we talk about your job?'

I don't understand how you actually network, as in how to actually do it."

Students are generally not taught this skill at all. It's just a phrase that's thrown around, but there's no real meaning or understanding as to what's involved. Young people don't know what it means to be good at it or how it actually helps them. The other part is that when they do start to realize what's actually involved in effective networking, they can get easily overwhelmed by it. They're afraid they're not good at talking on the phone, so they don't want to call anybody. They are afraid of speaking to a group or introducing themselves to someone new at events because they don't know what to say.

Some get as far as sending someone in their field of interest a message and receiving one back, but they have no idea where to go from there. To the new graduates who say, "I've been networking. I've been talking to alumni," I'll ask, "What are you saying in those conversations?"

"Oh, I just asked them for advice, but I didn't hear back." Or, "They said they were going to introduce me to someone but nothing came of it."

Young people have not been trained in how to direct a conversation to get what they want out of it. Instead, they message professionals and say, "Hello, I'm Caitlin and I really need an internship. Can you help me?"

I myself get messages like this one as I am active on LinkedIn. I cringe. When they come in, I think to myself, "Why would I give you an internship? I don't know you."

It's like going on a first date—are you going to ask that person to marry you?

Of course not.

New grads don't understand that they need to go slow, build relationships, and **show the people they are reaching out to what's in it for them.** Help them *want* to talk to you. Sometimes, job seekers are simply way too in-your-face: "I need a job!"

I have so much empathy for hungry job seekers who feel like they're running at a brick wall. But trying to bulldoze through it just will not work.

SERGE'S STORY CONTINUED

Realizing that the investment banking path was unavailable to him after his graduation from Purdue, Serge took a bootcamp certification program to learn how to code Python. He had always liked solving problems and using analytics. Software was what he really believed in. Learning coding and programming enabled him to give life to his ideas. Serge realized he liked it a lot more than finance: "What I really love about coding is there's no limit. There is no one telling

THE NEXT GREAT STEP

me that you can go this far, or you can only do this much. You can do whatever you want."

There was no wrong way, there was freedom in the field and in the skill set. "I just liked it and I kept doing it more—and nobody could put any boundaries on me," he said.

Serge already had all the pieces he needed to land a great job. We just helped him tell his story about his ability to code, and how he'd discovered and grew the skill set, which gave him confidence. He used our Meeting Plan and took our guidance regarding refining his LinkedIn profile and overall approach to networking. And that's how he ended up getting a fantastic job in the suburbs of Chicago at a Fortune 500 company called Capgemini SE.

In the final interview with the company, Serge's interviewer didn't use the questions that we had practiced. Instead, he said, "Just show me what you've done."

He'd coded a mock Pac-Man game and was able to show what he'd done. This company didn't care about his GPA or his resume, they were impressed by his actual work.

"I wish I'd had this help in college," Serge reflected after our work together. "I would have liked to have a solid understanding of how to think about making a resume and making a plan, how to think about meeting preparation, and answer interview questions."

Even though he ultimately landed a technical role, Serge still needed general job search help along the way. "The main struggle I had while searching for a job was knowing hardly anything about networking, resumes, cover letters, and interviewing," Serge said. "My school curriculum didn't actually cover these essential skills, so I had no idea if what I was doing was right or wrong."

Today, Serge is happy. He knows what to do when it comes to job seeking—how to network properly and what specific skills to put on his resume. Perhaps most importantly, he is surer of himself and what he has to offer. His cousin is really happy to see him start a career, and his mother, who had been stressed for an entire year, is ecstatic. Furthermore, the skills he learned to land this first great job offer will stay with him as he seeks out future professional opportunities.

Passive v. Active Job Seeking

New grads say, "I emailed a person. I sent them a message, now I'm waiting." The passive approach to job seeking doesn't mean your new graduate is solely applying online. I might categorize their efforts as too passive if I hear, "I spoke to somebody last week. They'll call me back when something becomes available." Or, "I talked to a person at the career fair and they said I should apply, so I did. They haven't gotten back to me yet. I'm waiting."

Students do a lot of waiting and they feel that waiting is active. They believe waiting is part of their job. They worry about having too many open leads at a time and may not be sure if they are ready to be offered one of them.

That's fine—but new graduates are too careful. I have to remind them, "This is business."

So often, young people are waiting around and not talking to other people, telling their parents or other stakeholders, "I don't want to bother them. I don't want to intrude on their time or make them think that I'm too persistent or aggressive."

They're very fragile. I think they're afraid of rejection or annoying someone. They're so afraid that someone will say, "Why are you calling me?"

It's a big issue.

My company was growing and I was trying to decide if I might need some more advisors. I put out the call to my network that I was looking for somebody new. Perhaps five to seven people sent me their information. I interviewed two or three of them. To be frank, I'm a little disappointed that the top one or two candidates with whom I connected had not followed up with me. Because if they had, I probably would have hired one of them. I really wanted them to follow up—to let me know they were truly interested in the role we had discussed. I was thinking, "I want to hire them, but they didn't send me a thank you note." Here is the cardinal rule of job seeking: *send a thank you note*. I tell every young graduate, "If you don't send a thank you note, even one line, that employer won't know how interested you are in the opportunity."

Everyone is so busy, and **new grads don't realize that being persistent with people matters a great deal**. The question is, "What do you say in the second letter and the third letter and the fourth letter and the fifth letter, every single week?" A lot of times, I don't think our students are following up nearly enough.

One of my favorite phrases to use in the job search is, **"Please pardon my persistence."** I want new graduates to use that line because it's almost guaranteed that people will actually reply when they say it. When responding on social media, a new graduate can write something to a newer contact like, "If you don't think we should speak, just let me know and I'll stop contacting you." Nearly every single time, that person will reply. Persistent, polite contact makes all the difference.

Connecting the Dots

Young graduates need help. They're lost in a process with no clear guidelines or directions. They're getting advice—which is often inaccurate—from every corner of their lives. They don't know how to network or have fruitful conversations. Fortunately, most are ripe for coaching and full of unarticulated skill sets. It's just a matter of connecting the dots for an employer as Serge ultimately did with our help (see sidebar).

Before we dive into the Next Great Step process, we will devote a short chapter to the employer perspective—what they are looking for and where job seekers often go wrong in the interview process.

CHAPTER TWO KEY TAKEAWAYS

- Focus on quality over quantity in applications.

- A perfect resume does not equate to more job opportunities.

- Successful job seekers help employers *want* to move forward with them by speaking intelligently about how they can solve that employer's problems.

- New grads need to go slow, build relationships, and show the people they're reaching out to what's in it for them.

- New grads don't realize that being persistent with people matters a great deal: "Please pardon my persistence."

CHAPTER TWO RESOURCE:

How to Survive the Job Search—From Someone Who Just Went Through It

"So, we've finally made it—the summer after graduation! Although it's easy to get caught up in the excess free time and beautiful weather, for many of us post-grads, summer also indicates that it's time to ramp up the job search. As somebody who just landed her first post-grad job after graduating Northeastern University in May, here are five things that I've learned."

- Leah Otner, Northeastern University graduate, class of '21

To read Leah's takeaways, please visit:

nextgreatstep.com/bookresources

CHAPTER THREE

EMPLOYER'S PERSPECTIVE

SECTION 7:
"I Don't Want to Babysit These Kids"

Employers post jobs because they have a problem: either they need existing work done and don't have enough personnel in place to do it, or they're intentionally growing and planning for more demand for their goods or services. Companies hire when they need to increase their revenue, improve their offerings, or expand their reach in some area. Unfortunately, the biggest disconnect I see when I talk to employers of all sizes is that most young candidates don't look at the situation in this way. They don't see the big picture or how they might fit into it. Instead of figuring out a way to solve an employer's specific problem—by performing to increase revenue or meet an organization's goals—a new college graduate is often too focused on their own concerns: "I need a job and I can't find one!"

New graduates don't believe that they are qualified enough to solve a company's problems, or that they could make enough of an impact to even help. This is the major disconnect employers are grappling with when they contemplate hiring new graduates, and it makes them less likely to even consider candidates who are seeking their first full-time roles out of school. This hesitancy is hurting both new graduates' job prospects and the employers who need to hire more people.

The result is often underemployment on the part of recent college graduates, which can hurt them for years. Data shows the unfortunate impact of this disconnect on new grads in the real world. According to a recent report titled "The Permanent Detour: Underemployment's Long-Term Effects on the Careers of College Grads" created by the Strada Institute for the Future of Work and Burning Glass Technologies, 43% of workers in the sample were underemployed in their first job. As they progressed, "the cycle of underemployment became progressively more difficult to escape." Furthermore, "Starting in an underemployed position leaves graduates generally on weaker financial footing to start their careers. On average, underemployed recent graduates earn approximately $10,000 (27%) less per year than fully employed graduates." New grads who are underemployed in their first job are *five times* more likely to be underemployed five years later as compared to their counterparts.[10]

"How Can You Help Me?"

New graduates have this idea of, "I deserve it," when it comes to a nice job offer. But the working world doesn't function according to arbitrary ideas of fairness. The stereotype, which is based on some truth, is that many young people received a trophy for showing up or for being the best at competitions that had little to do with solving real-world problems. Now, they're stepping into a completely different arena in life and don't have the mindset to compete. In many cases, it's not their fault: universities are not keeping pace with what employers need. They're not teaching Google Analytics or client relations; they're not teaching outside sales, networking to expand business opportunities or landing page copywriting, they're not teaching negotiation, critical thinking, advocacy, fiscal responsibility, time management, or how to learn from failure. The skills employers seek change very quickly, leaving job seekers frustrated.

Have we taught our college students how to work on a team? Do they know how to fill a market niche? Can they optimize or use a customer relationship management system? Or, at

---

10 "The Permanent Detour: Underemployment's Long-Term Effects on the Careers of College Grads," Burning Glass Technologies and Strada Institute for the Future of Work, May 2018. https://www.burning-glass.com/wp-content/uploads/permanent_detour_underemployment_report.pdf Accessed Jan 18, 2022.

least learn to do so quickly? A recent *Wall Street Journal* article reported that automation and digitization is one factor driving the increase in skills requirements in postings for high-skilled workers.[11] Many new graduates aren't prepared.

Also, it's important to consider the idea of "fit." Not every job is good for everyone. Instead of being desperate for any job offer, it's important to understand what a company really needs and if your student or new graduate is a match for that. Should they be miserable in a job or internship with a fancy brand name? No. Taking a position at Goldman Sachs because it sounds impressive and then being miserable there is not good for your new graduate's overall career trajectory.

A job offer shouldn't be viewed as a prize. The questions a candidate asks and the message they relay should be about aligning with the hiring manager's thoughts about what they are looking for. It's about being able to read the interviewer, ask the right questions, and help them see if there's a real match.

Many students and new graduates say to their parents, "I did what you told me to do. You told me to go to college, which I did. You told me to get good grades, and I did." So, their thinking goes, *now is the time for my next trophy,* which in this situation, would be getting a good job or internship.

---

11   "Job Openings are at Records Highs. What Aren't Unemployed americans Filling Them?" https://www.wsj.com/articles/job-openings-are-at-record-highs-why-arent-unemployed-americans-filling-them-11625823021 Accessed July 19, 2021.

An unsuccessful post-graduation job search is, for many young people, **the first time in their lives they have come up short, the first time they have really failed when it matters.** When this occurs, many new grads get very extreme in their thinking. Instead of committing to changing their job research tactics or making slight adjustments in their self-presentation in interviews, they default to: "I'm never going to get a good job." They're very fragile and thus don't ask enough questions about how they can ultimately meet an employer's needs.

Job seekers at every level need to understand the problems the employer is faced with—they need to understand why that employer has this job opening. Why is there a need for this role? What are the results that the employer is seeking?

Students and new college graduates are, too often, only focused on their own success: "This would be great *for me*." No employer really cares about that, it can be a harsh world. A potential employer isn't interested in what a college graduate "deserves." It's business. They are thinking, "Would hiring this candidate be good for the company? Will this job candidate help us achieve our goals or make my life easier or simpler? How will this candidate add value to my business?"

First-time job seekers often do not understand this dynamic.

New Grads Lack Job Preparedness

Several recent surveys on job preparedness reveal that while students give themselves high ratings on this metric, employers don't share the same assessment. Nine out of ten graduating students said they were proficient in terms of professionalism and work ethic in a poll of over 4,000 graduating students, yet only four in ten employers said the same, according to the National Association of Colleges and Employers *Job Outlook 2018* report, which polled mainly Fortune 1000 companies. A separate 2016 report from PayScale found the same thing: 87% of graduates thought they were "well prepared" to enter the workforce, but only half of managers agreed.[12]

Employers want candidates to come in and be good communicators who can *think*. They want job seekers who can write effectively, follow up, and have a sense of urgency when it comes to completing tasks and meeting goals. During an interview, HR professionals are assessing a candidate's level of critical thinking skills, as in: "Are you analyzing everything? Can you look at the entire picture at our organization?" as opposed to having an attitude of, "My job is to move this file from here to here and then I can go home."

Employers need people who can fit in and understand how their role might impact other people. **This is why internships during the college years are so important: real working experiences help new graduates ask the right questions and build a frame of reference.** New grads are often not matching their skills or self-presentations to what the employer's actual needs are, but that doesn't mean they don't exist. According to a recent Association of American Colleges and Universities'

---

12   D'Orio, Wayne. "Are Grads Ready to Work?" Human Resource Executive: April 11, 2018. <u>Are Grads Ready to Work? | HRExecutive. com</u> Accessed July 19, 2021.

report, liberal arts skills are valued and sought out in the workplace—contrary to what many think. Breadth and depth of learning are both needed for effective long term job performance. Completing active and applied learning experiences in college gives job applicants an advantage when it comes to getting hired.[13]

Our Turn: Employers Share Their Perspective

"I do not care if applicants come with specific experience or industry knowledge," said Nancy Josephs, CEO of Veritext, a national court reporting company. "I care that they have good communication skills, that they are analytical, and that they have drive and ambition. I can work with raw talent and move them forward but I do assume that candidates have the basic technology skills of understanding MS Office and similar software."

"I am willing to give people a shot," Josephs added. "But they need to show the desire to work, learn, communicate, and show they are easy to work with. I also expect that most candidates will want to change jobs within eighteen to twenty-four months as people tend to believe that the grass is greener elsewhere. I don't mind some turnover to get some new ideas. However, when picking a candidate, I would prefer they come to me for their second job, not their first. This is where an internship could work as a first job as

---

13   Flaherty, Colleen. "What Employers Want," April 6, 2021. AAC&U survey finds employers want candidates with liberal arts skills but cite 'preparedness gap' (insidehighered.com) Accessed August 6, 2021.

well. I want to know that they have transitioned from the academic world to the working world. They don't have to work in the exact job or industry, but they do need to show me how it relates to the position I am hiring for."

Adam Schneider is the father of four college graduates. He himself graduated from MIT, and is a partner at a strategy house Oliver Wyman, a Wall Street executive, and was previously a partner at Deloitte for more than twenty years. He has hired many students into big consulting firms and into the financial industry. Schneider recently shared his valuable insights with me about the disconnect between new grads' expectations and the reality of securing—and succeeding in—their first full-time role: "Most new hires do not understand that it's not like getting an A in class. Joining a firm is not a four month class, it's about a 10 year run to get to a senior role in consulting, a partner. New grads come in very smart but frankly are not that capable. They are also unproven, and the newest have the least experience. They have less value than they think they have. They need to learn what has to happen in the business, but they don't know the drill. For example, they typically don't understand the apprenticeship process in consulting.

"There is a lack of understanding of the success criteria," Schneider said. "Of course, they may have worked, but they've likely never worked full-time, on their own, before. Even in consulting, they may have had a summer project but not a serious, long term, 'this is a big deal' project where client expectations are very high. It is often a sea change for them. There are lulls in the academic experience (summer, Easter break, etc.) so the continual need to pay yourself in your work experience is not something they're used to. It's a multi-year journey of learning."

"Many new associates come in and get discouraged quickly. They complain, 'All I do is PowerPoint.' They don't realize that the content, the thought, and the structure of that presentation is critical for them to learn. This shows the gap between their expectations and what actually happens. Often when they arrive, they get discouraged quickly and quit within one or two years. And that is a shame—in consulting or finance, the roles and projects get much more interesting once you have some experience or have demonstrated your capabilities."

Schneider prefers to hire someone who has worked during college with an internship or other job because it shows that they have already had exposure to a traditional work environment. He is also more interested in candidates who are hungry for a career—someone who understands the value of being a partner, for example, and who has the energy for the role.

Skills and interpersonal fit matter as well: "If we are filling a tech role, the candidate needs to be tech savvy," he said. "If it's an HR role, they need to have strong interpersonal skills. For a strategy role, they must think past the obvious and solve problems. Minimal information comes from their GPA and school record, classes often have prescribed answers. In almost all roles we need someone who can *think*."

Finally, Schneider is looking for **candidates who can differentiate themselves by highlighting an evident work ethic.** He has three pieces of advice for young job seekers:

1. Help me understand your goals. Putting "president of the investment club" or "investment banking club member" on your resume and then saying you want to be a consultant is silly. Be prepared to *explain* to me why you want to be a consultant, because it sure seems like you want to be an investment banker!

2. Try to find the organization that has the people you want to spend time with (and can commiserate with) and a philosophy you believe in. It's all about the people: you are likely to be working crazy hours and spending a lot of time with them. Go with the people you like! If you don't like them, you won't enjoy the firm or the work. All there is in consulting are the people and there is an element of chemistry to pay attention to.

3. Be polite and careful. Write a thank you letter. Get the firm name correct. Make sure the interviewer's name and title is correct. Respond with a "what I learned" summary. Show a level of focus and effort that you would put into the work, should you get the job.

SECTION 8:
Why I Choose You Over Others

Young job seekers are often too general in their interview responses and too focused on the short-term. They'll say things such as, "I'm going to do this for a few years, see what I can get out of it, and then get a promotion." Their perception of how to build a career is inaccurate because of the way social media shapes the narrative. In that world, it seems like everyone is getting what they want so quickly. Most new graduates do not really understand the amount of work and effort that employees put into getting to that next level.

New job seekers lack self-awareness. They don't know what they have to offer, so they sound like every other candidate an employer interviews. Each person comes into an interview and says, "I'm so hard working. I will do a great job for you." Unfortunately, the next ten people who walk into the interview say the same exact thing.

Mike Zollenberg is the Chief Clinical Operations Officer at EHE Health. He interviews and serves on teams who hire candidates at every level of the company, from interns to doctors to C-suite executives. I recently chatted with Mike and asked him about his expectations when it comes to hiring younger job candidates for internships or entry-level positions. He first wants to see if they know about the company. "I'm always impressed when they've, at a minimum, read my bio and they come in having done some research," he said. "I wish [young people] knew that things aren't going to be handed to them. Kids think they know everything but they have to be willing to come in and learn. Talk about what you can bring to the company and why you want to work here. Ask, 'Where would I fit in here and how does this work?'"

Zollenberg said he likes it when candidates ask, "What do you like or not like about my background for this role?"

"I'm honest with them because they have to learn how to take advice and get real feedback from other people besides their parents," he said. "Find someone who can give you that feedback. Leverage who you know, any network you can. Continue to grow your network and stay in touch with people. I said this recently to many interns, students, recent grads or others: 'You have my cell number now. Text me, call me. I'm happy to help you.' But most don't call."

Employers have a hard time differentiating the people they're interviewing. The baseline is *every* college graduate is hard working and they're all going to show up every day at 8 a.m. Thus, employers want to know:

- What makes this person different?
- What skill set does this person have? Can they tell us or show us how they've used that skill set?
- Am I convinced this candidate really wants to work here?
- What has this candidate done or what will they do to help our business achieve its goals?

Employers are becoming more demanding because hiring and onboarding a new employee is very costly in terms of both time and money. In fact, the Society for Human Resource Management (SHRM) reported that companies spend an average of $4,129 per hire and take an average of forty-two days to fill a position, while a different study by the National Association of Colleges and Employers put the cost even higher—an average of $7,645.[14] Keep in mind, of course, that according to the U.S. Small Business Administration, hiring expenses involve more than just an employee's salary. The government agency says that a good rule of thumb is the cost per hire is generally 1.25 to 1.4 times the salary.[15]

Will This Candidate Be Easy to Train?

If a hiring manager picks someone right out of college, they will need to be trained and mentored and that requires planning, money, and resources. A lot of companies are not doing formal training programs anymore—they don't have the funding the way they used to. So, unless a job seeker goes to work for big finance, big manufacturing, or big pharmaceutical, for most companies, the training is on the manager, or on one of their staff. Everybody's trying to run lean, so it's an enormous effort

---

14 "The Right Time to Hire," America's SBDC New Hampshire, February 15, 2021. https://www.nhsbdc.org/blog/2021/02/right-time-hire Accessed July 26, 2021.

15 Weltman, Barbara, "How Much Does an Employee Cost You?" August 23, 2019. https://www.sba.gov/blog/how-much-does-employee-cost-you Accessed July 26, 2021.

of time, energy and money to do the onboarding—to teach somebody from the ground up. When people are making a hiring decision, that reality is a big part of what they're thinking: "Do I want to bring someone in that I can mold and teach the way I want, or do I want somebody more seasoned who already has some industry knowledge? It won't take as much time."

Everyone has a selfish interest. Employers are asking, "What makes my life easy? What makes my company more money? How can a potential employee add value? When can I start seeing the return on this new hire?"

Candidates right out of college create doubt in that employer's mind, because while they are enthusiastic, they are also often unserious and too vague: "Hey, what's up? How's it going? Oh my gosh, I'm so hard working, you should totally hire me!" This sort of self-presentation is a turnoff to an employer who has tough deadlines in terms of making their quarterly numbers. Instead of trying to bring a twenty-two-year-old up to speed, they need to be meeting organization-wide expectations *yesterday*. A manager looking for help wants to know that a particular candidate really wants to be there and understands their challenges because they've done the research. An employer wants a candidate who has a vision for exactly where they might fit in and contribute.

I have a very good friend who runs HR for a large investment bank. He recently told me they want candidates to come in and be specific about their goals (down to the department and role), because the people they interview are often all the same.

It's frustrating for the employer. He said, "I don't want you to tell me you want to be in finance when you graduate. I want you to tell me, 'I want to be in wealth management. I want to be in private equity.' I want someone to be really precise."

Is it fair for someone completely new to an industry or to the whole working world to know that? No, but it's what the employer wants. A new graduate may not know, but nevertheless, they cannot be vague and expect to walk out with a nice job offer. If a job seeker wants to have a shot, they need to do some homework on the website and pick one division that they like. We coach young job seekers to ask themselves, "Alright, if I had to go all in, what's it going to be and why?" Read up on why your skills are perfect for wealth management, for example, because that's how you will set yourself apart.

MY STORY

It was the spring of my senior year at Washington University in St. Louis in 1992, and I found myself jammed into a small office in the Career Services Center with fifteen of my peers. Our business school graduation was right around the corner, and this was the last rush to secure a job before we left. We were waiting for our interviews with the recruiter from Procter and Gamble (now known as P&G), for a coveted Consumer Products Marketing role.

As a marketing major, I felt obligated to apply since the position had the word "marketing" in the title. I really had no idea what the job was, nor did I want to move to Cincinnati, but I figured if everyone else in my class was interviewing, I should too. I didn't research the company, I didn't research the people. (You couldn't go on LinkedIn at this time, of course!) I probably could have gone to the library and looked up a periodical, done a little more legwork, but I didn't care because I didn't even know what to want when it came to my first "real" job.

Every candidate at the interview that day had the exact same resume, more or less, on our school-provided template. Not only that, we were all wearing similar gray or navy suits. At the time, I thought this should be enough preparation. I would rely on the 4 P's of marketing from my classwork (place, price, product, and promotion) and share how my strong academic record would make me a good candidate.

The first question my interviewer asked was "So, why do you want to work in Consumer Products?" I stuttered and gave a general answer about how I used Proctor and Gamble products. I mean, who didn't? They made soap! I fabricated another general answer about how they were a market leader. It went on like this for a while because I had been lazy and had not done my research, nor had I clearly thought through what skills I could bring to the company as a new hire.

When I had the opportunity to differentiate myself, I said the one thing everyone else had said: "I'm a hard worker and I'm responsible."

Nothing in that statement sets anyone apart. Not thirty years ago, and not now.

As expected, I did not get the job.

One of my friends was better prepared and articulated her value to the company. She has since built a successful career there. I continued interviewing and ultimately landed a sales role with a tech company in New Jersey. In that job, I was rarely asked where I went to college or what my grades had been. In fact, some of my most successful colleagues did not have prestigious degrees or exceptional transcripts—but they knew how to close business and make money for the company.

It was that simple—and a lesson to remember.

SECTION 9:
The Good News: Employers Need Recent Grads

Despite the challenges and concerns employers have about this cohort, new graduates *do* have value in the job market. Work needs to be done. Roles need to be filled. Employers might want someone with new ideas or energy that someone in their mid-thirties doesn't have. Or they might want someone willing to work longer hours, or stay late, or do things differently. There's a tremendous opportunity for employers to find some great talent in new graduates. There are a lot of employers willing to give entry-level employees a shot—and I'm one of them. I had a young woman, Claudia, who was an intern recently and I absolutely loved her.

When I interviewed her, Claudia was so focused. Remember, no one likes the interview. No one—least of all the employer—has time for it. It's a problem that the employer has to deal with and it's taking away from their regular work tasks. It's exhausting. It's hard trying to truly get to know someone in an hour.

With this in mind, this intern candidate said, "Let me tell you what I'm about." She was very clear about what her skills were, she was very clear about her aspirations, and she was very clear about what my company did. She said, "This is the research I've done and this is how I think I can help you."

In a few minutes, I was so blown away. Then, when I had her working for me, *she* organized *me*. Every week, she'd say, "Here's the agenda for our meeting." It just saved me so much time to not have to think about it or come up with something. She took care of it.

Sought-After Job Skills

LinkedIn analyzed millions of job postings across industries and identified the five most in-demand skills for anyone just starting their career:[16]

1. Analytical Skills

2. Project Management

3. Customer Service

4. Marketing

5. Time Management

Other sought-after skills or attributes include the pursuit of continuous learning, creativity and resilience, decision making abilities, experience collaborating effectively on projects, and emotional intelligence.[17] Employers want to hear about specific projects or situations in which candidates relied on these skills or traits.

---

16   Our 2021 Grad's Guide to Getting Hired. LinkedIn. May 18, 2021. https://news.linkedin.com/2021/may/our-2021-grad-s-guide-to-getting-hired Accessed August 3, 2021.

17   Omoth, Tyler, "The Top 13 Jobs Skills Employers Want in 2021," December 2020. https://www.topresume.com/career-advice/top-professional-skills-for-resume Accessed August 6, 2021.

Putting the Pieces Together

Companies want to hire people who have the desire to solve problems, who have the right attitude: "I'll do whatever it takes. If I don't know the answer, I'll figure it out—and I'll try to figure it out first before I come to you."

People just want to know: can you solve a problem at least somewhat on your own? Can you be resourceful? Can you be mature and adult and figure it out even though it's hard and uncomfortable and might take more hours than you think? Employers look for a strong willingness to work, to learn, and to be curious. Young job seekers have to clarify a skill they have and tell a story about how they've used it to demonstrate their competence in that skill. Employers get frustrated when candidates have no idea how their skills will serve them in the workplace. For example, they'll see someone who's an English major and wants a finance job (which is fine—there is actually a big push for hiring liberal arts majors in finance) but says something like, "I wrote nine papers last semester and got all A's. I think I want to invest for your clients."

That is not enough. It doesn't make sense. Writing papers doesn't connect to investing for clients. There has to be another component to what that young English major says, something like: "And in my spare time, I invested my own money, I read the *Wall Street Journal* every day, and I follow these stocks. This is how I would invest for your clients." Or, "I'm able to use my skills every day because I do a lot of reading and researching about the commodities market."

Young graduates have to put the pieces together. That's what an employer is looking for: people to make it easy for them to understand how they can help their teams and ultimately help their organizations.

Career services have recently reported brighter prospects for new college graduates as companies have adapted to video-based recruiting, new employee training, and employment. Adrienne Matarazzo is the Talent Acquisition Manager at Veritext, and she has good news for new grads: "We have had good success hiring recent college graduates into 60 to 70% of our roles at Veritext," she said. "They are trainable, moldable and they have the basic skill set we are looking for. Tech-savvy and good communication skills—those are the things we are looking for nationally."

CHAPTER THREE KEY TAKEAWAYS

- Employers post jobs because they have a problem that needs to be solved.

- Employers are looking for candidates that can demonstrate they can solve problems and add value to the company.

- Employers value internships during the college years because these experiences help new graduates ask the right questions and build a frame of reference.

- Everyone has a selfish interest. Employers are asking, "What makes my life easy? What makes my company more money? Who can add value?

- Young graduates need to be prepared for interviews, articulating their skills and differentiating themselves from other candidates.

CHAPTER THREE RESOURCE:

Creative Strategies New Grads Can Use to Land a Job

Recent graduates often assume the best way to find a job is to comb through online job boards and submit as many resumes as possible. This simply isn't true. Job board postings are extremely competitive and frequently lead to dead ends. Plus, they only represent 20% of the jobs that are out there. The other 80% are never posted online.[18]

To get these jobs you need to know someone or know someone who knows someone. You need to network aggressively. You want to avail yourself of every opportunity to meet people in your industry and sell yourself. You need to make sure people

---

18   Parris, Jennifer, "The Biggest Job Search Myth, Debunked" https://www.flexjobs.com/blog/post/biggest-job-search-myth-debunked/ Accessed August 6, 2021.

remember you. Imagine you're a recent graduate looking for a PR job. Instead of treading the path lined with ignored and rejected resumes, why not go a different route and use the skills you learned to help land a position? You could design a PR campaign to get your name out. Prospective employers will appreciate that you're demonstrating your skills in a novel way. You'll certainly stand out from the crowd.

To learn more strategies, please visit:

nextgreatstep.com/bookresources

THE
SOLUTION

GETTING STARTED

This section is designed to help your grad approach the search process in small bites. When you apply this simple, structured, step-by-step process, it will enable your grad to move meaningfully toward landing the job they want. Each piece of our process builds on the previous step, making the overall task of landing a good job offer more manageable.

You are welcome to flip to different sections to seek out answers to your immediate questions. However, if you follow this process sequentially, you will meet with greater success.

It consists of four key parts:

1. Define Success
2. Build a Strategy
3. Differentiate
4. Execute

Let's get started!

CHAPTER FOUR

DEFINE SUCCESS

SECTION 10:
Driving & Restraining Forces—
How Did We Get Here?

Many students or grads start this process feeling "less than." They are intimidated, afraid, and unsure of the path ahead. To move your own job or internship seeker forward, you'll need to meet them where they are. Do this by helping them understand their Driving and Restraining Forces. What are those forces, positive and negative, real or perceived, that push and pull on your student or new graduate and help them to determine where they currently are and where they want to be? This is the opportunity to start from scratch without judgment. I know this is difficult, but give them a chance to be honest without repercussions.

Below, you'll see a Force Field diagram to display this concept. According to this model, on the left side is 0% effectiveness, meaning nothing is going the way the job seeker wants. On the right side, you'll see 100% effectiveness, representing an optimal life. The truth is everyone is somewhere in the middle in terms of their current effectiveness and their current ability to accomplish their goals.

FORCE FIELD DIAGRAM

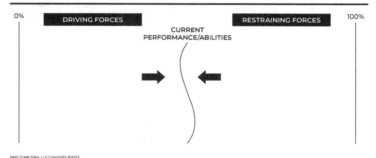

Next Great Step, LLC Copyright ©2022

Driving Forces

What are all of those amazing things that have enabled your student or new graduate to achieve success up until this point in time? Even though your child might think, "But I'm only a recent graduate," or, "I'm only twenty-one years old," the fact is they have abilities, personality traits, and skills that they have used to get them to where they are today, whether it's in academics, in sports, in the family, or in a volunteer organization. These are their Driving Forces: all things, internal or external, that have helped contribute to their success.

This is their opportunity to brag about themselves, to list the things they are good at. These are the skills they have learned, or the laudable traits they have acquired. These items can be strengths, insights, skills, attributes, or subjects in which your new graduate clearly excels.

We often find it's very hard for them to fill out this side, so don't be surprised if your graduate has a difficult time completing this exercise. It's challenging for young adults to stop and reflect on their strengths. However, once they get past their initial block, our clients find this exercise to be very empowering. It is the first step to move them forward.

Write Down Driving Forces

1. _____

2. _____

3. _____

4. _____

5. _____

6. _____

7. _____

8. _____

9. _____

10. _____

Restraining Forces

Next, you will ask your new grad to fill in the opposite side of the Force Field diagram. You want to know about those negative thoughts, weaknesses (real or perceived), fears, or challenges that your young job seeker faces. This is their chance to be honest with themselves. The new graduate completes the diagram on their own. Be prepared to learn that you, as the parent, might be a Restraining Force due to the expectations you place on them.

Write Down Restraining Forces

1. _____

2. _____

3. _____

4. _____

5. _____

6. _____

7. _____

8. _____

9. _____

10. _____

Below, you'll see an example of the kinds of phrases that often come up during this exercise. On one side are things like having leadership skills and being a hard-worker, but without fail, new graduates make the Restraining side of the diagram longer than the Driving side.

FORCE FIELD DIAGRAM

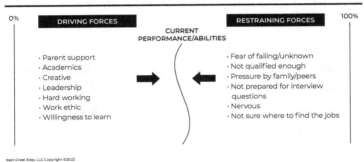

Next Great Step, LLC Copyright ©2022

Students and new grads often say things like, "I'm not good enough," or, "I'm not prepared, I'm very nervous. I have no idea what to do," or, "I can't find a job." This is all in their minds—it's their own opinion of where they stand but it's helpful to get these thoughts out of their heads and onto the diagram.

Weaknesses Become Strengths

The purpose of this exercise is to see the whole picture, yet realize it's just a snapshot in time. (On that note, we suggest that you have your new grad write the date on it for future review.) We understand young job seekers may feel lost and uncomfortable at the beginning of this process, but what we've also seen is that over the course of our time with them, we are able to move bullet items from the right side of the diagram to the left. For example, if a young job seeker says, "I'm not prepared for interview questions," by the time we finish teaching how to answer interview questions, this will be a strength of theirs, a Driving Force. While we can't change your grad's personality, or how they inherently feel about themselves, through this process we can change many items, like knowing where to look for jobs, how to network, and many other steps in this process. They're going to feel more prepared for interviews. They're going to feel more qualified by taking the time to define their skills. So, their list of Driving Forces starts to outweigh their Restraining Forces. It's a snapshot in time: *This is who I am, this is the way I feel right now.*

By starting here, it also helps us as advisors to know what our young clients are thinking and what's going on in their mind. It's a non-threatening exercise, there's no judgement and there's no right or wrong answer. **We as parents may think we could fill this out for our kids, but the reality is that we don't always know this information**. You may not realize, for example, how many perceived Restraining Forces your new graduate is wrestling with.

This Driving & Restraining Forces exercise came from my corporate consulting work. My team would meet individually with a CEO and ten executives on his or her team prior to our three-day engagement. We would ask each person: What are the driving forces of the business and what are the restraining forces?

Then, when we got everyone together, we overlaid all the answers so everybody in the whole organization could see which strengths and weaknesses were coming up repeatedly. From a business standpoint, it's an incredibly powerful exercise to have an assessment of what your own executives think. CEOs would often say things like, "Wow, I can't believe how many people believe that we don't have strong recruiting," or, "We don't have an up-to-date product."

This activity gets everyone on the same page and improves their understanding. It provides momentum to move forward.

SECTION 11:
Stakeholders—Who Cares?

Once they have an honest picture of their abilities, it's time to ask your student or new graduate about the people whose expectations are supporting them or weighing on them. These are their stakeholders. We define stakeholders as those people who have a vested interest in your new graduate's career success. As their parent or guardian, you are a stakeholder. These are all people who offer their opinion or advice regarding what your new grad should do with their career. Stakeholders are usually parents, guardians, professors, mentors, friends, family, etc.

Ask your new grad to list each stakeholder and what they think that person's expectation is for them in terms of a career. These expectations can press quite heavily on how a new graduate pursues opportunities in their search. Yes, this exercise sounds very business-y, but we know from experience that getting young job seekers to share thoughts about their stakeholders is useful. **These grads are getting advice and pressure from many different people: parents and grandparents, friends and professors—anyone who has an opinion about what they *should* be doing.** Sometimes, two parents are saying two different things and new grads are trying to balance that conflicting pressure with their own desires.

Stakeholder name: _____
Their expectation(s): _____

Stakeholder name: _____
Their expectation(s): _____

Stakeholder name: _____
Their expectation(s): _____

As you embark on this process, the idea is you want to understand what's happening in the background: what's going on in your new graduate's head, who's talking to and influencing your young job seeker and what they are saying. Again, stakeholders are all the people that are talking to your new graduate about their life, their success, their path.

I've had grads say, "Well, my mother just wants me to be happy, but my father really wants me to be a lawyer. And I have a professor who thinks I should go this other way. My friends want me to live in the same city as they do. The only stakeholder who isn't stressing me out right now is my dog!"

Doing this exercise helps them to see if everything is in alignment: "My list looks great and my parents are very supportive of whatever makes me happy." Or, there are times where the new graduate is able to clearly articulate some disconnects: "My parents really want me to go into this field or go into this job, but I'm not sure if that's what *I* want. These are the pressures and the stresses that I feel right now about meeting others' expectations."

No Right or Wrong Answers

Seeing these sentences written down can be quite eye-opening for parents because often, we don't know what our kids are hearing or feeling. During this part of the program, many students and recent grads have said to their parents, "Do you realize the pressure I feel? It's hard."

This is all good information for new grads to identify and for you as a parent to see. It provides a better picture of what's happening. Some new graduates are more worried about what their parents think than their parents may realize. Others care more about their sibling's opinions or about what their friends are saying.

There are no right or wrong answers. This exercise is simply meant to raise everyone's level of awareness and create open dialogue. **If your child decides to choose a path contrary to a stakeholder's stated wishes, that's fine. This is their**

opportunity to explore and share with you why a certain career choice is important to them. Whether they take each stakeholder's opinion into account or not is up to them. Potentially to your dismay, they may choose to ignore a stakeholder.

SECTION 12:
Vision—"What Should I Do with My Life?"

It's the million-dollar question: "What do you want to do with your life?"

In order for grads to figure out what they want to do in the next one to two years, ask them to think big and share their ideas and vision for the future. This can feel very overwhelming at first. Encourage them to brainstorm ideas regardless of what they studied or where they are right now. I know parents don't love to hear this, but during this part of the process, let go of what your graduate studied or what you thought they were going to pursue. Unhook them from previous expectations and let them *think*. Ask: **"If you could describe the future two to five years from now—not ten years or twenty years—what does it feel like? What might it look like?"**

The timeframe of this question is intentional because two years is a long time in a new graduate's frame of reference. Prompt them with these starter questions:

- Are you in a certain industry?

- Do you work with a large group of people, or a small group? Or are you working alone?

- Is there a title that you want to hold?

- Is there a certain demographic or city you want to be in?

Here are some additional questions to stimulate this conversation:

- What would it look and feel like going to work each day?

- What skills are you using?

- Would the company be large or small?

- Are there company names that you have in mind?

- Think big. Where do you *really* want to go?

Invite your new grad to think about their future without restrictions: *If you could do anything that you want, what would that look like? What do you see for yourself with the skills that you have?* We've gotten very interesting answers to these questions. Some young people are very specific: "I want to be the vice president of wealth management at Morgan Stanley." Others are vague: "I want to be creative. I want to be working with other people," or, "I want to be able to use my analytical skills."

Exploring these questions allows new grads to verbalize what they really want. It's okay if there's not a defined answer here; this is a starting point. The question is, **how often do we listen without jumping in?** Do we give our kids a chance? In many cases, parents are ready to offer help, suggestions, and forward along jobs they feel their children should apply for.

However, we don't often let our kids share their thoughts and feelings without bias and without the need to direct them.

Here are sample visions from Next Great Step clients:

> My hope in two to five years is to work at either a media publication or Hollywood-centric company related to pop culture media distribution. Under dream circumstances, this would be a company like Marvel Entertainment. I'd prefer to contribute to a product that most people consume as part of their daily lives.
>
> As for my role, I want to work in editorial but could also contribute to the writing side of production. This would include analyzing various scripts for spelling and grammatical errors, as well as determining which pitches have potential and which need work. I also hope the job would follow a traditional Monday-Friday work schedule but still provide room to work from home and take vacations over the holidays. However, my big hope for a future job is versatility. While I want to do something that feels emotionally and professionally rewarding, I'm hoping it provides opportunities to experience other sides of the company like marketing, distribution and production. By increasing my skills in these areas, I could do more in the company and take an active role in shaping its products. ~BW

In two to five years, I would like to work for a toy company of any size. It doesn't matter how big or small but the goal would be to work at Mattel. I would like to be part of the process of toy production from concepts and ideas, to designing and prototyping, all the way to factory production. I see myself working on my own individual tasks but being part of a bigger team that goes through the whole process together and as a team interacting with other people, departments or companies to work together to make the best product. I would first start off as just a team member, but in five years I would like to have more of a lead role in the team with the title of Project Manager. ~KSS

I want to be working in a lab environment in neuroscience/psychology. I want to be part of a small task-based organization or a medium sized company so I can always make a new friend, but won't be an anonymous face in the crowd. I do not want to do "busy work" for hours on end with music in the background. I want to work on a team but have the ability to break away and do my own work day-to-day. There are no specific titles I want; I just want to be a researcher for now. I don't want the responsibility of a manager or higher titles. I don't have any companies in mind because I am new to the field. I just want to make a difference in the world one way or another. ~EP

The Value of an Outside Perspective

As parents, we are fearful for our grads, and that fear colors what we say and how we listen. I don't write this with any judgment whatsoever—I'm at fault too when it comes to my own children. It's just easier for me to see the pattern because I'm talking to other people's grads every day and I don't have the same emotional attachment as I do to my own family. This perspective allows me to understand that it can be helpful for our kids to have permission to take a breath and think. Invite them to actually share what they want even though it might be uncomfortable. We understand you spent or borrowed a small fortune in tuition money and perhaps you've just heard that they don't want to actually *do* what they studied for four years. **Let go of the fear and give them that chance to say it.**

SECTION 13:
Goals—Let's Narrow It Down

Once you've identified a new graduate's Driving and Restraining Forces, their stakeholders, and their vision, it's time to break these grand plans down into manageable goals. In other words, you want to give them steps they can take *tomorrow*. The vast majority of our program participants are eager to meet the goals we provide them in this part of our process because they've been struggling. They've suffered trying to secure a job offer their own way. Without a framework of clear steps, they've been applying to dozens of jobs online and getting nowhere. They feel lost and uncomfortable. Thus, as you guide them through the steps you've been reading about in this part of the book, your new graduate will likely start to feel relieved.

You will now translate a young job seeker's big vision for their future into small goals they can tackle. A new graduate may say, for example, "I'd really like to be in a creative field working with people." You make that vision possible by breaking it down into manageable pieces. To do this, ask the following questions:

1. What does it feel like to be successful?

2. How do you measure that? (Is it only financial?)

3. In the next two years, do you see yourself jumping around, or do you see yourself sticking with an organization and trying to build a career there?

4. What don't you want to do? What do you dislike?

5. What do you want to do?

Start the Conversation

To get this conversation rolling, you can say, "Imagine I'm walking down the street and bump into you several years from now. I ask, 'How are you doing? Do you feel you've accomplished the success that you were looking for?'"

Framing it this way gets the young job seeker to see what really matters to them:

- "Success is feeling really proud about the work that I'm doing."

- "Success is doing a job where I feel supported, fulfilled and appreciated."

- For this generation of job seekers, it's generally not about the money. Some will say they want to be financially independent, but more often they say, "I want to feel like I'm making an impact," or, "I'm helping to save the world."

This conversation allows young job seekers to think about what they want in a new way—as well as how to measure it. It puts them in control. They get to make decisions about this process and where it's ultimately heading. You are empowering them.

Next, ask them the other questions on the list: "How many experiences do you see yourself having in the next two years? Do you see yourself jumping around, or do you see yourself sticking with an organization and trying to build a career there? What do you *not* want to be doing?"

They'll often say they don't want to sit at a desk, but that's not what you're getting at with this question. Instead, you are searching for *specific dislikes*, such as: "Healthcare is not for me even though that's what my parents do." Or, "I'm not really great with numbers, so I don't want to do anything regarding bookkeeping or accounting." These specific answers are excellent because knowing what you *don't* like is equally if not more important than knowing what you *do* like.

You want your new grad heading down a path where they feel connected to the role they are seeking. This part of the process is about starting to narrow their focus. The young person might have had a family member who said, "I know about this great job in accounting and you're going to make so much money." But if they get clarity that they really are not into accounting, it allows them to say no without the guilt. Then they don't waste time pursuing something that won't work out in the long run.

Finally, discuss what they *do* want to do with probing questions like:

Tell me what specific jobs appeal to you.

- What have you seen? What have you tried?
- What are your friends doing?
- What's out there that looks interesting to you?

None of this has anything to do with a job that is posted online today or put in front of them. Instead, invite them to dig deeper: to think, read, and research what might be possible. *They* get to choose. If your child consistently answers these questions by saying, "I have no idea," invite them to unhook from what they studied or what they think they should do. Ask them to think big and remind them it is okay to share any thought or desire regarding what they might want to be or what they are interested in. If there are still no answers forthcoming here, that is alright. We'll revisit this again when we uncover their skills and core skills in the next part of the program.

Giving Them Their Goals

We have found over time that new graduates are often all over the place with their goals. Thus, it is helpful to actually give them a preliminary set of goals to start. They can add to the list if they want to. Here is a good template to start with:

1. Identify one or two trade journals, newspapers, or websites covering the industries you are looking at. Read these three times per week to be more informed about the areas you want to pursue.

2. Identify ten companies of interest to you. Research these firms on LinkedIn, Google, or other platforms and be prepared to share why they are appealing.

3. Identify ten people who have a job you want or are doing something that interests them.

It can be helpful for you to look for alumni who graduated in the last five to seven years. Do not contact them yet. Instead, list their names, titles, companies, and years graduated.

Moving forward by taking steps to explore interests, companies, and people is the key here. **Young job seekers or internship seekers need to get smarter. I think new grads forget when they come out of school that learning shouldn't**

stop. Because when they get an interview, someone's going to ask, "Hey, why do you like our company?" Furthermore, it would be helpful to know if a company they're interested in is actually going bankrupt. Maybe it's not smart to apply there! New grads tend to be very narrow-minded about what is out there. Guide them to expand their horizons and identify the actual companies and people doing jobs they're interested in by starting with alumni from their school. A bit later on in the process, they'll begin reaching out to these new contacts.

TAKE NOTE:

Use this area to record answers
to the questions posed in this section.

_____

_____

_____

_____

_____

_____

_____

_____

_____

_____

_____

_____

_____

_____

_____

_____

_____

_____

_____

_____

_____

_____

CHAPTER FOUR KEY TAKEAWAYS

- Encourage your grad to list their list Driving & Restraining Forces to understand where they are now and help them to move forward.

- While stakeholders' wishes play an important role in a grads life, ultimately your child may choose another path as this is their opportunity to explore and share with you why a certain career choice is important to them.

- By creating and articulating a vision, grads can start to narrow down some of their choices.

- Setting goals allows job seekers to take small achievable steps to help them get smarter about the industries and/or companies they may pursue.

CHAPTER FOUR RESOURCE:

How You Can Help

If you are like most parents, you are increasingly concerned about your student's employment during and after college. As a result, you have likely become more involved in your grown children's search for jobs and summer internships.

The involvement is understandable. You may feel anxious to get a return on your investment after four (or more) years of tuition, as well as get your child financially independent as soon as possible to manage any outstanding debt from student loans so they can move out.

To learn how to help—and not hinder—your student, visit:

nextgreatstep.com/bookresources

CHAPTER FIVE

BUILD
THE STRATEGY

SECTION 14:
What Skills Will They Bring
to the Market?

If your grad takes away just one thing in this entire process, this section is the MOST important one. We see young adults overwhelmed and intimidated by the search process because it's uncomfortable. They may have a vision or goals, but grads often try to get a job by doing things piecemeal. They will work on their resume or apply online, yet many of them lack clarity on their own skills or how to present them to an employer. There is a disconnect between what they are saying and what an employer wants to hear.

We solve for this disconnect by helping them to build a **strategy** that answers two questions:

1. **What skills** do they have to bring to an employer?

2. And, **who are they going to bring their skills to** in a very focused way?

Young adults need a plan: an actual strategy for securing that first full-time job offer. When approaching the job search with your new college graduate, help them develop a strategy by having them answer the above two questions. Exploring these questions with you enables them to answer the question "tell me about yourself" in interviews, AND it empowers them to apply for companies that can leverage their best talents.

Determining a young job seeker's skill set is such a crucial part of the overall process because skills are the foundation for the individual's entire job search. Most new grads think that what they should be doing, first and foremost, is applying to jobs. This is understandable, of course, but it's not the best move. **Until they know themselves and what skills they actually have to offer, they're getting nowhere applying to whatever jobs come along.**

Yes, figuring what they want to leverage in terms of skills takes time. This is the hardest and most important part of our program because it's all about building up a young person's self-awareness. Some new graduates will say they aren't good at anything or have nothing to offer, but that's absolutely not true. Everybody has something—something that they've done, accomplished, or learned that sets them apart from others.

Here, your new grad is taking the Driving Forces exercise they did previously and revisiting it with more thought. These are the prompts we use to draw deeper information out of each young job seeker:

- What am I good at?
- What do people tell me I'm good at?
- Where am I most competent?
- Where is my passion?

Have your job seeker create a list of the skills they think they can bring to an employer. These are both hard skills (writing, Excel, financial modeling, etc.) and soft skills, which are more like personality traits (trustworthy, responsible, etc.). When they create the list of their skills, invite them to think about a situation, assignment, or work project they can reference that demonstrates that skill. Have them make a brief note of that experience. This is important because it is not enough to say you have a skill, job seekers need to point to real experiences to show they know how to use it. Note that *skills are not aspirational.* If they claim they have a skill, they must be able to prove it with related experience.

Skills List

Skill: _____

Experience:_____

Skill: _____

Experience:_____

Skill: _____

Experience:_____

For example, if they add "writing" to their skills, they may want to reference how they wrote three articles a week for the school newspaper or wrote social media copy for a club or part-time job that led to an increase in followers or engagement.

SKILL FOCUS

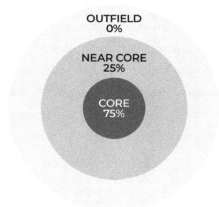

Core Skills

The next step is to narrow down a job seeker's list of skills into their top three. Core Skills are the things that they are *most* competent and *most* skilled at—the skills they actually want to use on a day-to-day basis. Though you know your new graduate has more skills than just three, it's helpful to focus on the core.

Secondary, or near-core skills, come next on the list and are the things that your job seeker *could* do but doesn't want to do all the time. For example, perhaps they're great at math, but don't want to be doing a mathematical role.

Finally, teach your young job seeker about the concept of the "outfield." The outfield is another word for the *shiny object syndrome.* This is what happens when someone comes to a grad and says, "I have a great job for you. You're going to make six figures, but you need to move to a town you've never heard of and do tasks you didn't set out to do." It's when someone gives your grad a compelling offer to secure a role that they had not considered, and does not fit within their core skills. For example, your child is looking for a public policy job in Washington, D.C. because they want to get involved in politics, but someone in their network needs a social media marketer for a startup in Silicon Valley and they are tempted to go for it. Or, they want to work in the music industry, but someone offers them a guaranteed commercial real estate job. Your new grad could do the job, but it's not what they were looking for.

The outfield is full of distractions: it's what they *do not* want to be doing—and there's nothing wrong with that. Categorizing things in the outfield is helpful because outfield opportunities take time and focus away from the core, which is where new grads need to spend their energy. Outfield opportunities generally do not align with Core Skills. Our experience has shown that people who pursue outfield opportunities end up leaving these roles, feeling unfulfilled, and starting the job search again from scratch.

Think of allocating your skills in terms of percentages: you want your young job seeker to spend 75% of their time, effort, and energy focusing on opportunities that leverage their Core Skills. Guide them to spend perhaps 25% of their time considering roles that would tap their near-core, or secondary, skills. *You don't want them to spend any time on outfield items.* Sure, someone can always pursue an outfield job, but if a particular job seeker is saying they love sales, writing, and doing research—yet the job they're looking at doesn't leverage any of those three skills—they're wasting time and energy. Any time spent on outfield opportunities takes time away from where their true focus should be—on their Core Skills.

Identifying Core Skills helps job seekers do a few things. First, it provides the framework to answer the question, "Tell me about yourself." No matter who your new grad is talking to, they'll always know what their Core Skills are and will be able to frame their answer around these skills. Second, identifying their three Core Skills helps your graduate to be very clear and concise later on in the interview process. When a young candidate is nervous, they tend to ramble on. If a job seeker names too many skills and rambles, they'll often be passed over for a job. This methodology helps keep them on track. Finally, identifying Core Skills allows the young job seeker to focus their job search.

Core Skills

1. _____

2. _____

3. _____

The Power of Three

There is a reason we ask young job seekers to narrow down their list of Core Skills to just three. People have short attention spans, and most can't remember more than three things. This principle goes all the way back to the philosopher Aristotle, who wrote about "the rule of three" in The Rhetoric.[19] The power of three even appeared in the pilot episode of Schoolhouse Rock![20]

---

19   The Rule of Three | 2015-03-02 | Quality Magazine Accessed September 15, 2021.

20   www.throughlinegroup.com/2016/04/10/why-three-is-the-magic-number-for-interviews-and-speeches Accessed September 17, 2021.

Identifying your graduate's three Core Skills requires them to narrow down a larger skills list by thinking about the stories they can tell about using a particular skill in real life. If you want your job seeker to go one layer deeper, ask them to think about the real needs of employers in their field of interest as well.

Hard Skills v. Soft Skills

As you guide your new graduate to define their Core Skills, help them determine whether their list is full of hard or soft skills. Hard skills are the things that are easiest to measure. Ideally, we want your grad's Core Skills to be hard skills, those that have been taught or that are measurable. Soft skills are the opposites; they are more like attributes. For example, your graduate may be very responsible, hardworking, and timely, all of which are commendable, but those things won't differentiate them in the job market. Instead, these words describe *how* they did the skill: "I was able to solve this problem because I showed up on time and have great attention to detail." Showing up on time means very little, of course, if you can't actually solve a problem.

Guide your new grad here to ensure they don't say their skill is being hardworking, responsible, or trustworthy. Presenting these traits as skills is a wasted opportunity to share a more valued skill that helps differentiate themself as a candidate.

Employers seek hard skills such as:

- Problem Solving
- Leadership
- Communication
- Analysis (Financial/Data)
- Marketing
- Social Media Content Creation
- Research
- Writing
- Graphic Design
- Public Speaking
- Technical Knowledge
- Computing Skills
- Critical Thinking
- Teamwork/Collaboration
- Creativity
- Negotiation

Developing a Skill Story

The next step is inviting your young job seeker to answer two questions: **"How are you going to sell your skills? How did you demonstrate that you have that skill?"** Guide your new grad to give a summary of a time they used the skill: maybe it was a class they were in, or an internship they had. To tell a strong story, ask your job seeker to be very specific about the challenge they faced when they used a particular skill and how they overcame it.

We developed this proprietary framework for a Skill Story to showcase a skill in a simple and effective way. Superior to the STAR method for behavioral interviews (Situation, Task, Action, Result), our technique focuses on the challenges and accomplishments associated with specific experiences. Our method tells an interviewer how they used their skill, how they are competent at it, and how they can use that skill again to benefit the employer. Our technique focuses on the challenges and accomplishments associated with specific experiences.

SKILL STORY TEMPLATE

1. Summary of my position (title/company/class)

2. Tasked with (assigned responsibility)

3. Problem/challenge/difficulty

4. How I solved it (how I applied my Core Skill)

5. What I accomplished (measurable impact)

To start, your grad needs to think about an experience that presented a challenge and how they solved it. They need to focus on exemplifying their Core Skills in this process. This experience can come from many places - a work experience, summer internship, college coursework, or campus involvement. It should be from college or afterwards, not a high school experience unless it was highly unique.

You can brainstorm with them, especially if they have ever voiced a previous incident where they may have struggled. The concept of the Skill Story is to identify the difficulty, highlight that challenge, and then explain how you dealt with it. While each client we work with has their own unique stories, here are some common themes we hear repeatedly:

- Lack of experience or training
- Assignments given with tight time constraints or little guidance
- Too much information/not enough information
- Teamwork dynamics/Classroom dynamics
- Learning about a new industry
- Learning about a new tech platform
- Customer service experiences

Once they have decided which challenge they will present, they need to show how they solved that problem. This is the heart of where they prove they used that Core Skill to accomplish their goals. This part of the Skill Story will vary a lot depending on what your graduate's skill set is. For example, "I used my knowledge of Excel and v-lookup tables." Or, "I talked to people who use the database to figure out what information they never referenced." Or, "I delegated responsibilities to my teammates based on their strongest skills."

The final part of the story is them conveying what they accomplished for the company or organization or group as a result of their effort. While many new grads often think that learning something new should be their accomplishment, it is not compelling to an employer. A much stronger response would be "I helped the company narrow down their database to 300 qualified, strong leads. The sales team was able to pursue those leads and as a result, they acquired three more clients in Q3."

The following (image) represents a complete Skill Story:

SKILL STORY EXAMPLE - ANALYTICAL

My role was an Intern at Intronis which provides cloud backup and data security.

I was tasked with analyzing sales data to identify historical trends of clients who might buy our products in the future.

The challenge I faced was that this data had not been reviewed or analyzed before. The sales team needed qualified and accurate information.

I solved this challenge by researching 3 databases and utilized excel v-lookup tables to identify trends. I compared and analyzed the data and presented a summary of findings to the leadership team.

As a result of my analytical skills, the company was able to target 1000 new potential prospects. This resulted in **20 new clients and 5% increase in revenue**. I feel confident in my ability to analyze complex sets of data while supporting company goals.

Here are a few other examples of complete skill stories:

Core Skill - Problem Solving

"I worked for a pizzeria delivering food to local customers. I was tasked with figuring out how to deliver food to clients while keeping my distance during the early unknowns of the pandemic. Clients were afraid to have any contact while signing a receipt, coming to the door, or handing over a tip. The problem I faced was how to deliver the food and complete the transaction while making sure the client was comfortable. I addressed this in two ways: by calling the customer when I was five minutes away and letting them know when the food would be on their front porch. I also suggested to the manager that the order takers on the phone should ask the customers how much they would like to tip the driver, so that no contact was needed. This idea was implemented and used at the pizzeria for months. As a result of my problem solving skills, I created a streamlined procedure for deliveries which resulted in clients ordering more often and ensured that the restaurant was able to remain profitable. I am confident I can use my skills to solve problems for your organization."

Core Skill - Writing

"My role was a social media intern at a beloved local ice rink. I was tasked with getting more engagement on our primary social media page. The challenge I faced was the existing page for the facility had very little content. I solved this challenge by researching and writing a series of ten profiles of the rink's regular customers, focusing the short pieces on what they loved most about skating at the rink every year. Each person shared the features on their own feeds, increasing the organic reach of the ice rink's page. As a result of my writing, page views increased 20% month over month."

Refining the Story & Getting it Right

As you can see, an effective Skill Story is a hard-hitting collection of four to eight sentences. New grads are not used to talking about themselves in this way. They have to practice though, because once the Core Skills are figured out, everything in the search process becomes easier: the targeting of companies, the interviews, the letters. Every piece of the job search comes together around a clear focus.

This is the bread and butter of the entire process and getting this right is hard. It's not quick; refining their Skill Stories takes a couple of weeks. In most cases, no one has ever guided your new graduate to approach a job search like this. Career Services at most colleges and universities do not have the capacity to help hundreds or thousands of students get their stories clean.

How to Refine Your Grad's Skill Story

Sometimes, a young client will write their Skill Story and our coaches help with revisions. Sometimes it may be a good story, but it may not be a good fit for describing that particular skill they were highlighting. For example, they may have been showcasing their analytical capabilities, but their story was more focused on project management.

We may re-categorize a story because the skill a young job seeker initially chose just wasn't the right descriptor. That's ok, it's a process. We apply our own critical thinking to what new graduates are presenting.

To do revisions with your own recent graduate, have them read the story out loud to you and evaluate the following questions:

Does the story they tell match the skill they've defined? Or could it work better for a different skill?

Does it make sense? Is this skill truly a strength and relevant to their search?

Are they concise and easy to follow?

Learning to Tell the Story

To recap, ask your job seeker to:

1. Create a laundry list of all their skills.

2. Give proof of experience to narrow down the bigger list to three Core Skills.

3. Compose three Skill Stories (one per skill) following the format you just reviewed and have them practice saying them aloud.

The following week, role-play so your job seeker gets more comfortable telling their Skill Story without having to refer to their notes. You can prompt them: "You shared that you have expertise in analytics. Tell me about a time when you used your analytical skills."

Here, they are creating the answers to the test, or in their case, the interview. When you ask this question, your young job seeker may look alarmed. **While they can read the story if it's a phone interview, it's important for them to get comfortable telling it off-the-cuff. This is hard for them but there is no way around it: when you're talking to somebody, you need to be confident in what you are going to say.** This process is the foundation for the Next Great Step method.

Practicing helps. Guide them to improve their public speaking skill set: looking people in the eye or into the camera, working on their voice, and intonation.

Ultimately, you want your new grad to have more than three Skill Stories. Job seekers should have two possible stories for each Core Skill. If they tell you that they're great at problem solving, for example, there should be more than one time in their life when they used that skill. They might have a primary Skill Story about working on a group project and how they solved a problem in that context. But if I'm interviewing them, chances are very good I'd love to know another story as a backup. It could be about how they resolved a problem amongst friends or in their neighborhood. When they get into an interview, the questions sometimes repeat themselves and they don't want to have to say the same answer twice.

Many new grads are not thinking of the big picture when it comes to their job search. They're just asking, "Is this job good for me? Will I get the most out of it?" It's time to teach them to approach this process from the opposite perspective: **It's not about the job being good for the job seeker. It's about *them* being good for *the organization* and having the skills that could add value to that organization.**

SECTION 15:
Who Will They Bring Their Skills To?

When new grads first start our program, they often say they'll work for anyone and do anything. While this sentiment is completely understandable, it's now time to invite them to focus on particular geographic regions, specific companies, and actual people. If your new graduate wants to work in technology, for example, encourage them to get more specific, as in, "I really want to work for Cisco, Oracle, or Apple."

Who wants your grad's skills? How do they bring these skills to the right people? Once a new graduate has clarity on their Core Skills and their Skill Stories, it's time for the next step in this process—figuring out which people and companies are of interest to them and reaching out to those individuals. After your job seeker has their Skill Stories written and has put a good deal of practice into verbalizing them, ask:

- **Where are you going to take these stories?**

- **Who wants these skills?**

You want your job seeker to start thinking about where these people are and what companies they work for. Fortunately, they've already started this process. In the beginning, during the Defining Success portion of this work, you set the goal for your job seeker to create a list of ten companies and ten alumni they were interested in. Now it is time for that initial effort to expand. Hopefully they've been doing some research already.

Have them start by listing their three core geographic areas. Next, guide them to list three industries and five specific companies:

Geographic Areas:

1. _____

2. _____

3. _____

Industries:

1. _____

2. _____

3. _____

Companies:

1. _____

2. _____

3. _____

4. _____

5. _____

The key during this step is to remind your new graduate **they have control over where they decide to bring their skills**. Thus, they need to do some deep thinking and research about where they'd like to work. The job seeker is the captain of the ship and they decide where to go. This thought process starts with a geographic region or specific list of cities. From there, they narrow it down to three industries. Then, to five companies. Finally, they start to find the people inside these companies they can eventually meet.

Think, Research, Track

After your grad has done some deep thinking about who they'd like to work for, it's time to start keeping track of these potential contacts and opportunities. We have a Job Tracker tool in Excel for our clients and invite them to get more involved in using it by making some lists of actual people. They might begin by listing all the industries or all the companies they like, but eventually you want them to narrow it down to specific people with whom they can connect.

The following page is an excerpt from our Job Tracker Tool:

NETWORKING CONTACTS

Date Entered	Contact Name	Company Name	Alumni (Y/N) and year graduated	Date connected on LinkedIn	Date follow up letter	Date of first meeting/call	Date Thank-you sent
10/04/2018	Example: Joe Smith, VP of Sales	Ketchum, ad sales	2012				

Let's explore exactly how this is going to work. Encourage your new graduate to begin with those they already know, the people in their circle from school, volunteering, work or internships, then move on to alumni from their school. There's a feature on LinkedIn that helps users find alumni called the Alumni Tool.

This feature contains many filters. They can search for people in a specific graduation date range, major, and geographical region. For example, if your student graduated with an English degree in 2020, they may want to see who graduated from 2014 to 2019 with the same major, currently working in the greater New York City area. They can even use industry keywords. This is how your job seeker will start creating their list of people to reach out to.

Once your job seeker fills in a small database of interesting contacts, ask them to actually make a connection with them. How do you get someone who's on that list (who they've never met) to agree to be their connection? Perhaps the only thing your new grad has in common with them is that they went to the same school. The good news is that getting a person to accept your job seeker's request is not as difficult as new graduates think it is. We give them examples of how to write a compelling note of introduction. As research shows, adding a personalized connection letter like the one below increases the likelihood that someone will ultimately accept a new connection. This gently nudges your young job seeker into the process of creating actual contacts.

Here is an example of a note:

INTRODUCTION NOTE

Sam,

I am a fellow Penn Stater studying Journalism and Media Relations. I just completed an internship in digital marketing at SBC Marketing and am looking to expand my experience. I am interested in learning about your role as an Account Manager at VaynerMedia and your career path since graduating. I appreciate you connecting.

Best regards,

In most cases, if your graduate writes a friendly note, people will accept their connection request. Then they can send another message in LinkedIn, or via email now that they have the person's email address.

FOLLOW UP LETTER TO SCHEDULE A MEETING AFTER CONNECTING

Sam,

Thank you for connecting on LinkedIn! As I mentioned previously, I am a journalism major at Penn State. I have experience in digital marketing and am looking for an internship that leverages my digital marketing, writing, and sales. I am very interested in learning more about your role in account management and how you progressed in your career. I would like to speak with you via phone or in person for 20 minutes. May I suggest times A, B, or C to meet? Let me know and thank you again! I really appreciate it!

Best regards,

With this note, a job seeker is asking for time to talk. The idea is to create an opportunity for an informational interview (which will be covered in detail in the next chapter). When they do the follow up, guide your opportunity seeker to stick to a very focused message: "As I mentioned, I just recently graduated. I'm looking for a job that leverages my skills of digital marketing, writing, and sales." Note that the job seeker's Core Skills are clearly presented in how they now communicate about themselves.

Creating a Strong Elevator Pitch

Get your new grad into the habit of incorporating their Core Skills every time they communicate. Each job seeker needs a strong and concise elevator pitch that features where and when they graduated, their major or area of focus, and their Core Skills. Here is a template, and an example:

ELEVATOR PITCH TEMPLATE

I'm a YEAR OF SCHOOL/RECENT GRAD studying MAJOR/MINOR at COLLEGE/ UNIVERSITY with a concentration in AREA OF FOCUS. I have strong skills in the areas of CORE SKILL 1. CORE SKILL 2 AND CORE SKILL 3. Specifically, I just finished an internship/volunteer role at COMPANY/ORGANIZATION WITH RELEVANT EXPERIENCE where SAY WHAT YOU DID IN ONE SENTENCE. I am looking to leverage my skills in TYPE OF ROLE YOU ARE INTERVIEWING FOR at an organization like yours – specifically because of your focus on COMPANY FOCUS/ COMPANY NEWS. I look forward to learning more about your organization.

SAMPLE ELEVATOR PITCH ANSWER

I'm a Junior studying Electrical and Computer Engineering at Washington University with a concentration in Signaling and Embedded Programming. I have strong skills in the areas of problem solving, communication and coding. Specifically, I just finished an internship at Telegrid where I developed embedded signaling for security systems used by the military. I am looking to leverage my skills in a hardware design role at an organization like yours—specifically because of your focus on cybersecurity and wireless technology. I look forward to learning more about your organization.

Invite your new graduate to practice this pitch aloud to friends, family, and the mirror. Record them. Often, they initially feel as if they ramble on too much or that they could do better. They may not sound as smooth or as prepared as they want to sound, but that is okay. Keep it positive; this process takes practice and patience.

Having a well-thought-out elevator pitch sets the job seeker up for success for the rest of a meeting. If your new grad does not have an internship they can reference, they can discuss a key project from a class or a volunteer role on campus. By highlighting their Core Skills, they give the interviewer the chance to ask targeted questions about their experiences. Remember, the goal is to make it as easy as possible for the interviewer to know what to ask of them—and how they can ultimately add value to their organization.

Companies Need New Grads

When they first start putting feelers out on LinkedIn, new grads are often pleasantly shocked to find people are receptive to their overtures. If they're not making new connections, I'll ask a new grad how many requests they sent out. If I hear *three* I challenge them to send another five or ten out every day. When it comes to networking and making connections, they need to cast a wide net. This is where they should be spending their time—not aimlessly or randomly applying for jobs on job boards. If they see a job online that they like, they've got to make a connection with an individual at that company before applying. LinkedIn is a good first step for doing this.

Generally, young job seekers find that the people they reach out to actually reply and are quite friendly. They can't believe that people are willing to talk to them—but the fact is, companies seek fresh talent! New grads are trainable and they have the skills employers want. Companies need new graduates.

How Are You Feeling?

As we work with new grads, we check in often with them to see how they feel about the work we're doing together. As you go through this process with your own graduate, check in with them now. What do they feel is working? What's not working? Have empathy if they express doubt.

During this part of the process, the initial feeling is often skepticism. They sometimes don't understand why we spend so much time on Skill Stories. New grads are a little impatient because they all want to move fast, meaning they want to apply to more and more jobs. They want to know why they aren't sending out applications and working on their resume.

Fortunately, job seekers start to see why what we are doing makes sense when they finally get their story right. Once they nail it down, we ask them how they feel. At this point, they usually say, **"Actually, that felt really good. It sounded good; I have a strong story."**

We understand when we first talk to a student that they hope our process will be quicker than it is. Initially, some grads may feel that our process is cumbersome and could be slowing them down. Before long, however, they have that "AHA!" moment when they actually do the work and see the value of the exercises we have gone through. We record them, they see themselves, and we give them feedback. The clarity they have when they talk about themselves and their experiences using our methodology is a complete revelation. They begin to feel genuinely confident.

Of course, we don't let them rest at this point. It's time for them to start connecting with people on their contact list and scheduling networking conversations. This step seems intimidating but if someone replies, then it feels good again. We're trying to give them that positive reinforcement, but what's nice is that *they've* done it. **They are creating results**

THE NEXT GREAT STEP

for themselves. You didn't do it, you just gave them the tools.

As they put in the effort, they're gaining confidence: "I know my skills and people actually replied to me. I know what to say when I first talk to someone. I know how to introduce myself." All of these pieces are self-esteem builders. Before, all of these job seeking tasks felt overwhelming. We break it all down into manageable pieces. We have had clients who, after getting their Skill Stories figured out, have gotten job offers quickly. But most new grads need time. It could take eight to twelve weeks to get comfortable with this process. It just depends on where they are in the process when they start, and how much work they put in once they engage with it.

CHAPTER FIVE KEY TAKEAWAYS

- Until they know what skills they actually have to offer, students and recent grads get nowhere applying to whatever jobs come along.

- By creating a Skill Story, they can demonstrate their experience in a concise and efficient manner to show their value to an employer.

- Grads need to be comfortable telling their Skill Story off-the cuff. This takes a lot of practice - but when they are talking to somebody, they need to be confident in what they are going to say.

- Grads need to bring their skills to the right companies and people. By narrowing down the geographic areas, industries and companies they start to focus on the right opportunities

- A strong elevator pitch highlighting Core Skills sets the job seeker up for success.

Optimize a LinkedIn Profile

Your new graduate's LinkedIn profile is valuable online real estate. This platform provides an ideal place for them to connect with, and get to know professional contacts. Be sure your graduate takes the time to make their profile as strong as possible. To do so, encourage them to complete their entire profile and pay particular attention to the *About* section.

Here is a resource on how to maximize the entire profile and enhance your About section for best optimization:

nextgreatstep.com/bookresources

DIFFERENTIATE THEMSELVES

SECTION 16:
The 3 A's Meeting Plan

Grads start to gain confidence when they understand their skills, but now what? How do they use them to start moving their search forward? It starts with a conversation—over the phone, via video, or in person. The goal here is to create an impression or impact on the person they are speaking with. This is an opportunity for new grads to differentiate themselves. The key here is they should not "wing it." *Every* interaction they have as part of the search process should have a plan. We call it the **Meeting Plan**.

We recommend using a Meeting Plan for *every* interaction that a candidate has with any connection in the search process.

This could be a twenty-minute "get to know you" phone call, a planned networking session, or a formal job interview (more on this in Section 22). The magic of creating a Meeting Plan is the idea that a job seeker can **take control of their interaction and direct it to achieve a specific action such as moving further along in the hiring process.**

The heart of the Meeting Plan is a unique concept, **"The 3 A's."** It's how a new graduate can structure the conversation. **It's a strategy: convincing someone that there's a problem and that** *they* **are the one who can solve it.** This three-part approach enables candidates to know exactly where they want to take the conversation and how they can share their unique value in the process.

THE 3 A's

ACTIONS What you want the other person **to DO** or agree to do after the meeting or call.

ATTITUDES What you want the other person **to BELIEVE** about you at the end of the meeting or call.

ANSWERS What you want to find out from the person. What **QUESTIONS you need answered**.

The First A: Action

Before the young job seeker has their meeting, ask them, **"If everything went incredibly well during this conversation, what would you like the other person to do, or agree to do,**

for you?" Many say, "I hope they like me." or "I hope they answer my questions." This isn't a strong enough outcome. Here, you're looking for the job seeker to describe an action such as, "This person will introduce me to the Hiring Manager and ask them to meet with me later this week."

It's *that* kind of action you will guide your young job seeker to aim for, as opposed to, "I'll get back to you," or, "I'll review your resume." The whole point of developing a Meeting Plan is to keep the end goal in mind. **The job seekers want the person they're meeting with to be compelled to take a meaningful action afterward that moves them further along the process of securing an actual job offer.** Challenge your young job seekers to think about the end game: "You haven't met this person and they don't know you. What's the best possible thing that you could have them do?"

Example Actions:

- Introduce me to the hiring manager
- Introduce me to a current employee
- Arrange for me to shadow an employee for the day
- Agree to meet again
- Hire me

An important note: only one Action needs to be accomplished to have a successful meeting. It's also important to be aware of what Action is appropriate to ask for based on the timing and who the job seeker is meeting with. If it's the first time they are meeting with a contact, the Action of "Hire me" is probably not appropriate.

The Second A: Attitude

In order for that person to do something concrete and agree to take an action they have to *believe* something about your job seeker. You want your young job seeker thinking, "What do I want that person to believe about me as a result of our conversation today?" This is where their Core Skills and Skill Stories come in. Before the meeting or phone call, a professional contact just sees a new job seeker as a resume. They don't know that your new college graduate managed a project or is highly analytical. They don't know that they brought in 5% more revenue to a company during a part-time internship. Yes, that information is on your new grad's resume, but most people are very busy and won't have read it. So, the question is, **"What attitude do you want them to come away with from the meeting that will compel them to take action?"**

Example Attitudes:

- You can create compelling copy to increase the number of clicks/follows.

- You are technologically current on multiple social media platforms.

- You can analyze client requirements and customize content to their target market.

- You are adaptable and can communicate effectively.

These are the words or phrases your grad wants to hear from the contact. These types of statements affirm that they "believe" the skills and the stories the job seeker has told. They see how the seeker's Core Skills can be applied in their business.

The Third A: Answers

The last piece in the planning is to keep in mind that every meeting is a two-way street. Job seekers are not only being evaluated by their answers to interview questions, but also by the type and depth of questions they ask. Consider what answers a job seeker needs to assess the opportunity.

Example questions to seek Answers:

- How do you measure success for a new employee?
- What qualities would help someone be successful in this position?
- What skills did the previous person have for this role? Why were they successful or not?
- Can you tell me about the company culture?
- What are the greatest challenges you are facing in your department?

These should be consultative questions to seek information, not about basic facts that can be looked up on Google. This is how a job candidate can understand what the expectations are at a particular organization and what it would be like to work there.

PUTTING IT TOGETHER

Meeting Plan Template - completed prior to meeting

Actions: What do you want the person to do at the end of that meeting that will get you further along in the process? (Your goal is to get them to commit to at least one.)

1._____

2. _____

3._____

Attitudes: What do you want the person to *believe* about you? (These are your three Core Skills, with a brief example of each.)

1. _____

2. _____

3. _____

Answers: What information do you need to understand the opportunity better? (Have at least three questions ready to ask.)

1. _____

2. _____

3. _____

4. _____

Sample Meeting Plan

Actions:

1. Introduce me to the hiring manager.

2. Introduce me to another employee who's doing the job I'm interested in so I can learn about it, or perhaps come in and shadow them for the day.

3. Agree to meet with me again in thirty days.

Attitudes:

1. "You can increase the number of clicks on the website and we really need that right now."

2. "You're able to analyze client accounts and make recommendations. You understand our needs and can help solve our problems."

3. "You've created visually appealing materials, and I can see how your skills would benefit our department."

Answers:

1. How do you measure success at this company?

2. What are the qualities that help someone be successful in the role?

3. What did the previous person do in this role? Why were they successful (or not)?

4. What are your current challenges and priorities?

5. What is your time frame for making a hiring decision?

SECTION 17:
What They'll Actually Do in a Meeting

Planning vs. Executing

To review, the job seeker *plans* the meeting in this order:

1. Actions
2. Attitudes
3. Answers

However, the job seeker *executes* the actual meeting in reverse. It wouldn't make sense to walk in and say, "hire me" or "introduce me" without laying the groundwork first. Getting the opportunity to ask your questions first is like getting the answers to the test. This will allow job seekers to then structure what they share about themselves in a way that aligns with what they know success looks like.

Thus, the actual meeting flows like this:

Introduction/Share Agenda

1. Answers
2. Attitudes
3. Actions

Closing

Introduction & Closing

Every Meeting Plan will have an introduction and a closing. A job seeker starts by introducing themselves and setting the agenda for the call. This could be a version of their elevator pitch.

SAMPLE INTRODUCTION

"Thank you for meeting with me. To recap, I am a recent graduate from UT Austin who studied digital marketing with a concentration in web design and public relations. I am looking to leverage my skills of writing, analytics, and digital design at an organization like yours—specifically because of your focus on client solutions. For our call today, I would like to ask you a few questions about your career path, tell you a little bit about myself, and then discuss possible next steps. Does that work for you?"

This approach is effective for networking and informational interviews because that person wants *the grad* to have a plan as they are generally too busy to run the call. Therefore, a young job seeker needs to come in totally prepared and say, "Here's what I'm going to do today. I'd like to ask you a few questions about your career path, tell you a little bit about myself, and then maybe we can talk about next steps."

During the closing, your grad should summarize:

- What they learned
- The skills they can apply to the role
- The Action that the contact agreed to take
- Time frame to follow up

SAMPLE CLOSING

"I learned that your priority is to launch a new product in the US market. I am confident my skills of analysis and writing can support you in the effort to get to market faster. As discussed, you're going to email Sally to share my resume and I'm going to follow up with you in two weeks. I appreciate your help."

When a young job seeker prepares and manages the interaction this way, they have presented themselves as organized and ready to help a company achieve their mission and, thus, helping the person they are speaking with see them as a problem solver and a serious candidate.

Why This Works

When you teach this concept, it can be difficult for your job seeker to put it all into motion. This is different from how they have been interacting with connections in the past. **Our whole philosophy is *if you don't ask, you don't get.*** People are willing to help them if they are focused, articulate, and clear about the value they can add. When a candidate makes a specific request, it's clear to the contact how to help them. People are happy to help if you are specific on what you need from them.

A common concern here is about what happens if the meeting does not go well. Or if the contact is not willing to take an action. Even in these cases, the meeting was not a wasted effort. First, the ability to practice the "3 A's" and get comfortable with speaking to new people always helps future conversations go better. More importantly, the grad has now made a connection and can build on this relationship, even if there is no opportunity right now. Thus, their default request should always be, "Can we stay in touch?" or, "Can I update you on my search?" or, "Can I seek out your advice as an expert in the field as I pursue my search?" Very often, this person can become a mentor and provide guidance on the industry or future connections. Meetings will not always go perfectly, but the connections are what matters.

When a job seeker follows the "3 A's," it shows them that **this is how people get hired.** A job seeker truly differentiates themselves when they say, "I think my skills could really help your department accomplish its goals. You said your focus is on achieving 20% growth this year, and I feel confident that I can help you exceed that." Once a job seeker focuses on the numbers and works out a measurable metric to share, they come across as a confident individual who can and will help an organization solve its problems. Even when there are no specific metrics, if a candidate can show how they can positively impact a business, this approach works.

Using the "3 A's" at Networking Events

New college graduates can take control of any meeting with a professional contact, whether it is an actual job interview or a casual chat with a person they've just met at a career fair or a networking event. When the meeting is less formal because there are a lot of people around (and they only have a minute or two to talk with someone), they can still follow the "3 A's" plan. It's just an abbreviated version of everything we've reviewed in this chapter. A job seeker can start by saying something like, "Nice to meet you. I'm a recent grad from Penn State. I was a Journalism major and I'm looking for a role in Marketing Communications in the healthcare industry." They must give a short version of elevator pitch and then ask the person they've just met about themselves: "Tell me about you. What's your role? How'd you get into that position?"

It's all about asking questions and truly listening to the answers. Sometimes people think so far ahead about what they're going to say that they miss good information. Encourage your new graduate to slow down and listen during networking events. Then, guide them to ask questions that make sense: "What do you do as a project manager? That's something I actually thought about pursuing myself. How did you get into that role? What do you like about it?" Being curious is so valuable when they're networking. Finally, a new grad should wrap up the short three minute conversation by saying, "I'd love to talk with you more. Can we exchange information?"

One, they provide a little pitch. Two, they ask some good questions, and three, they find a way to follow up: "I know we don't have a lot of time here. Can I get your information so I can follow up with you?" Then, they can reach out later that day or within twenty-four hours. Networking conversations are simply a compressed version of the "3 A's." Be curious, and follow up quickly.

SECTION 18:
Standing Out

How did that candidate get chosen for the job? What did they do differently from the rest? Parents and grads have answers such as, "the right major," "a strong GPA," or "family connections."

Performance during the live interview is a key indicator of why a candidate gets selected. Let's look at two candidates, Joe and Ryan, who make it to the final round of interviews, and explore why one gets the job over the other. These two candidates went to the same school, have the same major, and have the same GPA.

An employer asks, **"Tell me about yourself."**

Joe says, "I'm a recent grad from Wisconsin with a communications degree. I enjoy working with others and have experience working as a team member in group projects and as a leader in the advertising club. I had an internship last summer where I helped write press releases for a media company. I am excited about this opportunity at your company and would like to learn more."

Ryan says, "I recently graduated from the University of Wisconsin as a Communications major. I have strong skills in the areas of writing, communication, and digital media. Specifically, I just finished an internship at Edelman where I wrote copy for three campaigns for a Fortune 500 tech company. I am looking to leverage my skills in a digital media role at an organization like yours because of your focus on the client experience and focus in the technology sector. I look forward to learning more about your organization."

Which answer is more compelling?

Joe's answer is absolutely fine—but it's also vague and the impact Joe made in his experiences isn't exactly clear. Ryan's answer is clear and concise. There is also a tone of confidence in knowing who he is and what he wants. It's easy to understand how he made a good impression.

Candidates can also differentiate themselves with their answer to this question, **"Why should we hire you?"** They should be prepared to say the answer whether they are asked this question or not. Joe says, "I am a hard worker and trustworthy. I am excited about this opportunity and I think it would be great for me in terms of my career growth. I really like this company and I know I can be a good fit."

Ryan says, "I understand that the company goals are focused on improving your social media presence with clients in the technology sector. By leveraging my writing and digital media skills, I can contribute to attracting more clients in this sector. I demonstrated this in my work at Edelman and on campus in the Future Business Leaders club with my marketing expertise. I know how to collaborate with team members to complete a project and will be focused on helping your company achieve their goal of 10% year-over-year growth. **I am confident** that my skills of writing and digital media can contribute to impacting your bottom line and I am excited to start on this initiative immediately."

Which one would you hire?

The example with Ryan shows an understanding of his own skills, how these skills can help the organization, *and* ultimately how his efforts can help a team impact the firm's bottom line. Sounds tough to a twenty-something, but it's easier than they realize. It's about how they can put themselves in the shoes of an employer. Graduates often tell me they worry they don't have the credentials to apply to a job. They worry about competing against other graduates from better schools with better grades. Employers worry about themselves and how they achieve their goals. The more your job seeker can make the employer's life easier and help them be successful, the more they will want your candidate—regardless of their grades or degree.

Thus, urge your job seeker to proclaim, "I can do this. Let me tell you how." Guide them to use the word *contribute*: "I can contribute to reducing the costs of bringing in more revenue," or, "I know your goal is X percent growth and I feel confident my skills would contribute."

This not only needs to come across in an interview, but also while networking, and through written correspondence. This approach transfers to the resume as well because people want to see metrics. People don't remember all the words they read but they do remember numbers. And they may interview multiple candidates in one day. Therefore, it's wise to get to the point, and to use metrics to help them remember your experiences.

A CANDIDATE DIFFERENTIATES THEMSELVES WHEN THEY:

1. Listen, and demonstrate that they have done their research by understanding company goals, culture, etc.

2. Have clarity on their own skills and show how these skills apply to helping the business succeed.

3. Focus on helping the company achieve its targets and metrics—most importantly, helping them solve their problems. It's all about adding value.

Above all, even having the right language to communicate your value to an employer is not always enough. The positive way it is communicated to a connection or potential employer is paramount to the execution. We are empowering grads to have confidence, but equally important is to be respectful and show true excitement about the opportunity.

"Some of the things that help us to separate two candidates with very similar profiles," says Talent Acquisition Manager Adrienne Matarazzo, "are personality, professionalism, and ENERGY! A candidate's enthusiasm to become a part of our organization is what we want to see during the interview process. We want our new hires to be excited about joining Veritext and that starts at the very beginning. Recent college grads are sometimes limited in the area of work experience, so we rely heavily on personality type to determine who the best fit would be for each role. In fact, this is sometimes considered the most important qualification, especially for our client-facing roles."

Practice

When a young job seeker sees the "3 A's" Meeting Plan, they often say, "You're kidding, right? I actually have to say this and do this?" In one sense, they're feeling great about their skills. They have started reaching out to new contacts on LinkedIn or over email and they're experiencing some wins as people get back to them. But now it's time to actually have those meetings, and it intimidates them.

If a young candidate feels scared, a practice session is in order. Work through a Meeting Plan together. Next, guide them to pick someone to contact who isn't the most important phone call, someone that they just want to try it out on. For example, they can get their feet wet with a fellow alum who might have a similar job to the one they want. It doesn't have to be a big thing, and it's not going to be 100% perfect right out of the gate.

That first meeting a new grad schedules with someone they connected with on LinkedIn is not going to be the most beautiful conversation they've ever conducted. Still, they have to try it using our framework. Even if part of it goes right or they get the person to do something at the end without even telling them their Skill Stories, it's a win.

Young job seekers are often a little frightened and timid when it comes to executing a Meeting Plan and knowing the value they bring to the table, but this piece of our process gets easier with practice. We're telling them to reach out and start making these connections, and soon afterward, people do reply to them. New grads say, "I have no idea what to say when we get on the phone!" But that's the point of having a Meeting Plan—*we're telling them what to say.* **Practicing is the easiest way to be ready for the call or meeting that matters most.**

People hire people, so your new grad can't avoid talking to people if they want a job.

CHAPTER SIX KEY TAKEAWAYS:

- Job seekers must use the Meeting Plan for every interaction - taking control and directing it to achieve a specific action.

- They want the person they're meeting to be compelled to take action afterward that moves them further along the process of securing an actual job offer.

- The philosophy of the job seeker should be, if you don't ask, you don't get.

- The main way a job seeker stands out is by demonstrating VALUE: by showing how they can solve an organization's problems.

- Practicing is the easiest way to be ready for the call or the meeting that matters most.

CHAPTER SIX RESOURCE:

Here are some strong questions to ask to get ANSWERS:

1. Tell me about your role. What did you do early in your career to help you get there?

2. What are the greatest challenges that you face in this role?

3. How does your company measure its success?

4. What advice would you offer to someone starting out who wants to get into this industry?

**For more guidance and tips on how to
Ace a Virtual Career Fair, visit:**

nextgreatstep.com/bookresources

CHAPTER SEVEN
EXECUTE

SECTION 19:
The Resume - Isn't That All They Need?

Everybody thinks that if they just fix their resume, they'll be fine. Young people put so much effort and energy into this particular tool because they believe it'll solve every problem: "If my resume is great, I'll have all these wonderful jobs," or, "Then, people would find me," or, "If I have all the right keywords and all the right things in place to beat the tracking system, I'll be great."

This kind of thinking is a huge mistake because it's just not true.

A resume is one small piece of a very big puzzle. In our program, we work on resumes at the end of our process and a lot of our young clients get quite frustrated by the delay.

The reason we're not doing this task at the start is that this document has to be an *extension of the job seeker*—it's not the product itself. Think of it like this, a job seeker has a brand, a way that they want to represent themselves. This brand conveys the skills and value a job seeker can offer. The resume is just a tool to support the candidate. It's NOT what ultimately gets them hired.

Candidates don't realize that **what they *say* carries more weight than any resume.** Of course, people do use resumes as a screening tool, but interviews are really more important as a filter. Even if an HR person picks your new grad on the basis of the information on their resume, to get hired they will still have to verbalize their skills and communicate with ease.

People assess candidates based on who they like and connect with. They're asking themselves, "Could I work with this person? Do I resonate with what they're saying? Are they well-spoken? Do they talk too fast?"

It's definitely not fair. But this is how humans tend to judge job candidates—on their skills and how they communicate. As a parent, I have so much empathy for young people who struggle in this area. It's not always a transparent process and it's based on incomplete information. But the important thing to understand is that when young people who are not articulate, or aren't good at talking to a camera try to get a job offer, **their resumes cannot save them.** Yes, a resume is important and necessary to optimize the guidance you'll read in this chapter; it's just not as important as most job seekers think it is. It's not the one thing they need to get hired. However, a resume is necessary. Here are our tips on how it can best reflect a candidate.

Resume Checklist/Format & Content Tips

1. Formatting – Use black text and keep the font size and style consistent. Use bullet points, be consistent with punctuation at the end of each line, and don't include a lot of descriptive text. Ensure dates are in the same format and aligned (right justify the date and location). Keep the resume to one page. The exception to this is when applying for technical roles and including a separate relevant project sheet.

2. Contact Info – Use a contact email other than a university email address. It should be professional and clearly state their first and last name if possible, e.g. joe.smith@gmail. com. Avoid nicknames such as gamerboy@nyu.edu or coffeelover@umd.edu.

3. LinkedIn URL – Include under the name. Create a custom URL on LinkedIn that only shows the name, not the unique ID they assign.

4. Online Portfolio – Include links to any online portfolios for creative or technical backgrounds (i.e., GitHub, Behance, etc.).

5. Education – State the school, degree, and highlight the major. Include GPA (if over 3.0), graduation date, academic honors, and relevant coursework. If there is a work history of a few years, move this section below relevant experience.

6. Skills – The main content in each of the job descriptions should highlight the job seeker's Core Skills. If these skills are Problem Solving, Leadership and Analysis make sure the descriptions on their resume back these up and include the actual skill words. For example, use "Analyzed and implemented a new process that decreased the error rate from 5% to 2%."

The most important thing to keep in mind as you help your job seeker refine a resume is simplicity. This one-page document should be clean and easy to read. Leave out the colors and the fancy graphics, even if they are a graphic design major. Many resumes are read digitally; therefore, complex fonts and graphics won't be picked up by e-readers that are searching for keywords only. Guide them to create an online portfolio if they're in a creative field, so they can show off what they've done in terms of photography or design. If they're a writer, have them consolidate all of their pieces and make it easy for someone to go to a website and find examples of their work.

Remember, *people do not read and they do not listen.* A job seeker needs to present something that is easy to understand in a few seconds. In a quick glance, the reader needs to see right away where the candidate went to school and what they studied. Make it easy for others to find the job seeker on LinkedIn.

Skip the objective statement. In general, I don't think new graduates need it. A lot of them say, "My objective is to find a position that will help me to grow." It sounds hokey. Unless you're an executive and your objective is to be the CFO for an organization, this statement is not necessary and is out of style right now. The more years they're out of school, the less important this is.

When it comes to work experience, only include relevant experience. I understand new grads may not have any, but if they delivered pizza, scooped ice cream, *and* worked at a law firm, they don't have to put those experiences in chronological order. Place the work experiences that are most relevant on top. A resume is yet another place where the job seeker can take control. Experiences don't have to be listed in a time-based order. Instead, the order should be based on relevance. We often recommend job seekers title their experience as "relevant experience." This will allow recent grads to include key projects and assignments that may be directly relevant to the work they are seeking but are not work experience. This becomes especially important when recent grads may not have direct work experience in their field. Have them remove any high school jobs or clubs unless it's relevant to their field of interest.

Metrics and Action Verbs

People read for numbers. They need metrics to get a sense of what a job seeker has accomplished. So, instead of them writing, "I helped deliver pizza," guide your new grad to include information such as, "I delivered over $5,000 worth of pizza over an eight-week period to 20 customers." Yes, it's the same thing but the second sentence sounds better. It shows that the job seeker is aware that as an employee, they understand how the business worked, and how they helped it make money: "I wasn't just delivering pizza, I actually impacted this business and helped it to grow. Week over week, I was able to make 20% more deliveries than my coworker."

Guide your graduate to be consistent and concise throughout. There's a Google formula for presenting skills that we encourage young job seekers to use: "I accomplished X as measured by Y by doing Z." *I grew revenue by 10% by mapping new software features.* For each work experience they include, be sure to convey:

1. What did they do?
2. How did they do it?
3. What was the impact?

I recently had a young client who was really clever with an example like this. He said, "I optimized my delivery route. I was always mapping and making sure that I was not overdriving, because time is money."

Whether the candidate was a leader or whether they volunteered, how they explain it matters. Many people still say, "I was responsible for…," but *responsible for* doesn't express what a job seeker actually did. **Every sentence on a resume should have a strong action verb:**

- Built
- Created
- Analyzed
- Developed
- Collaborated

In addition to the above, we share a list of power verbs with our clients and encourage them to use those to convey each relevant work, volunteer, or leadership experience. Here are a few of them:

> Chaired, Coordinated, Executed, Headed
>
> Programmed, Implemented, Negotiated
>
> Spearheaded, Founded, Accelerated, Improved
>
> Delivered, Integrated, Standardized
>
> Refined, Simplified, Transformed, United
>
> Guided, Fielded, Informed
>
> Assessed, Tested, Measured, Investigated

Where the Core Skills Come In

The reason your job seeker spent so much time developing their Skill Stories is so they can complete a key piece of their resume. If they're telling you that one of their Core Skills is analytics or analysis, guide them to *use that word in their resume:* "I analyzed this process and decreased the error rate by 10%." Make sure they're being consistent in their brand. **This is why it's important for the young job seeker to create their Skill Stories *before* creating their resume.**

Here is a good example of an effective resume. There are metrics throughout, the action verbs are all aligned with the candidate's Skill Stories, the formatting is clean, there are bullets, and you can see numbers:

Beth SampleStudent
1 Main Street
Livingston, NJ 07041
beth@nextgreatstep.com
www.linkedin.com/in/bethsamplestudent

EDUCATION
Penn State University, Smeal College of Business   University Park, PA
B.S. in Marketing   Expected May 2019
GPA 3.5, Dean's List
Relevant Coursework: Marketing Strategy, Organizational Behavior, Sales Management and Strategy, *Management Capstone*

WORK EXPERIENCE
Kappa Search Inc.   Wayne, NJ
Marketing Intern   May 2017-August 2017
- Supported 3 clients to complete 12 marketing campaigns to grow local presence.
- Collaborated with Vice President to analyze 80 different marketing metrics for 3 clients that measured the success of each campaign.
- Designed a new intake process for prospective clients looking for social media support.

Jeff Lake Day Camp   Stanhope, NJ
Senior Counselor   June 2016-August 2016
- Supervised and led 22 eleven-year-old girls at a premiere NJ summer day camp over 8 weeks. Directed a Junior Counselor and Counselor-In-Training to support the eleven-year-old girls' group.
- Provided leadership to campers in all areas and acted as a role model in camp activities teaching the values of sportsmanship, rules, and peer relationships.
- Supervised and ensured the safety of 18 boy and girl campers ranging in age from 4-14 years during the hour bus ride to and from camp each day. Implemented daily programming.
- Communicated with parents regarding children's medical or behavioral needs.

CAMPUS/COMMUNITY ACTIVITIES
Beta Gamma Sigma Honor Society   September 2017-Present
Membership Chair
- Recruited and initiated new members to join Business School honor society.
- Built strong presence on campus by representing chapter at campus-wide functions and promotions.
- Planned and executed 2 membership events to attract new members.

Atlas THON – Penn State Dance Marathon   September 2016- Present
Donor and Alumni Relations Chair
- Raised over $2000 in funds individually for annual drive to benefit pediatric cancer.
- Facilitated an outreach program to alumni that increased participation contributing to 20% increase in donations.
- Communicated with executive board members on fundraising progress and new donor initiatives.

SKILLS and INTERESTS
- Proficient in MS Office PowerPoint, Excel, Word; familiar with Mac & Windows operating systems
- Listening to music, grilling, managing own stock portfolio (4% higher than S&P 500 in 2016 Q3)

This sample resume is easy to read; it's easy to understand the candidate's school, major, and the fact that she had several strong work experiences.

A LinkedIn profile should be an identical replica of the job seeker's resume. Thus, if they're using LinkedIn as an initial means for communicating, they don't need to send someone a resume because they should be able to see all of this information right in their LinkedIn profile. Do not attach it as a separate file.

A young job seeker just out of school doesn't need a resume writer at this stage of life. They don't need to write this document from scratch, either. Instead, start with whatever they already have and guide them to improve it using all of the tips in this chapter. **A resume needs to be clear, concise, and easy to read. It's all about how the job seeker can make the hiring process as painless as possible for the person who has to evaluate them.** An employer does not have the time or the energy to truly get to know candidates. They're already stressed, because there is a problem that they are trying to solve by hiring someone new. Remember that.

SECTION 20:
The Cover Letter

New college graduates tend to have quite a bit of anxiety about writing cover letters. I'd like to use this section of the book to offer some comfort. By this point in the process, your job seeker knows who they are, what they want, what their skills are, and the value they'll bring to an employer. Therefore, writing a cover letter for a particular job opportunity doesn't have to be an ordeal. Have them follow the guidance in this section, use the cover letter sample provided here, and continue to reach out to people via LinkedIn who are connected to the particular jobs they're applying to.

Cover Letter Basics

- Have them submit both their cover letter and resume in PDF format.

- Each cover letter must be customized for each contact or opportunity.

- The cover letter should highlight their understanding of the company, the person's or company goals, and how they can help to accomplish these goals with their skills.

- Guide them to research the company to personalize the letter. Identify 1-2 key areas about the company that are interesting to them.

- Remind them to use their Core Skills to explain their value.

- They should use their experience to explain how they are a fit for this job opportunity. Do not just summarize their resume.

- Have them use KEYWORDS to make their letter stand out (i.e., problem solver, leadership, research, digital marketing, etc.). Highlight the key words they use in the job description.

- Find a specific contact person at a company, rather than addressing the letter to a "hiring manager" or "to whom it may concern."

- Use a business letter format, even if you are sending by email. This includes proper mailing address.

- Keep it to one page of three or four paragraphs. When in doubt, keep it short and use bullets.

- Proofread for correct grammar and spelling.

Build the Cover Letter

Opening Paragraph: You must engage the reader with an opening sentence that makes them want to continue reading. Use a quote, name a person who referred you to the job, or even an industry statistic. Avoid the classic phrase, "I am writing to apply for...," and make your letter stand out. Share with the reader the skills or experience you have to offer and how it helps to solve their problems.

Second Paragraph: Use your Core Skills and examples to explain how you can fulfill the requirements of the job. This is your chance to distinguish yourself from other applicants by demonstrating how you have used these skills previously and can apply them to this job. Instead of a traditional paragraph, you may also use bullet points to add emphasis to your letter.

Third Paragraph (optional): Analyze your background and add any additional relevant information about why you're a good fit for the company/role. This is your chance to address any appropriate explanations (i.e., why you are an English major who wants to go into finance, etc.), or your involvement in extracurriculars. If you felt you covered your points in the above, then skip this and keep it shorter.

Closing Paragraph: Recap your skills and fit for the job and share with the reader your contact information. State that YOU will follow up.

Cover Letter Example

Dear Ms. /Mr.:

BHG Corp. is a leading digital marketing firm that creates unique content to grow a client brand. Your strong record of helping clients achieve greater growth through your digital marketing campaigns is impressive. I have proven experience in the digital marketing space where I have created unique content and written copy on all social media platforms to grow followers and awareness. Also, my ability to effectively communicate contributes to client success. I am confident that I can support BHG Corp to accomplish its key goals in the Digital Marketing Associate position.

When looking for a Digital Marketing Associate, it is critical to find someone who developed compelling content while representing the interests of the client. Some career and education highlights that align with these core requirements include:

- As an Intern for the New York Red Bulls, I wrote 2-3 articles per week for the team website, created 7 new social media posts per week and analyzed results using Google Analytics.
- As a social Media Intern for the University of Wisconsin Hockey team, I wrote 4 articles per week for team websites, live-tweeted game activities, controlled team social media accounts, reaching up to 200,000 people across all platforms.
- For my senior capstone class, I developed a digital market campaign for Nike Running and successfully defended my approach of how to improve the Nike brand image.

I can add value to BHG by leveraging my leadership experience demonstrated at Washington University. Currently, I serve as the Marketing Editor of the Olin Business Review where I lead all marketing ideas and strategies to improve brand awareness on campus. I also contribute my time tutoring teens at a non-profit that helps them prepare for college.

Based on my ability to effectively generate unique copy, digital content, and successfully communicate with clients to meet their needs, I am a strong candidate for the Digital Marketing Associate position at BHG. I welcome the opportunity to speak about my qualifications with you in more detail. Please feel free to contact me at (973) 577-6161 or at beth@nextgreatstep.com. Thank you for your time and consideration. I will contact you next week to follow up.

Sincerely,

Your name

SECTION 21:
Interview Prep (Stop "Winging It")

There is a step between optimizing the resume and cover letter, and having an interview. When they come to this juncture, young job seekers are getting the opportunity to speak with real people in their field of interest. The question is, how do they prepare? The approach you'll give your job seeker at this stage is very tactical.

The information they'll gather here is important to know *before* they talk with anyone at a particular firm or organization:

- What does the company do? What is the company's mission?

- What is interesting to me about this company?

- Who's the company's CEO? What is its current stock price?

- What is the latest news that concerns this industry or firm?

- What in the job description does the job seeker like?

The person who will eventually interview your job seeker will want to know, "Did they read what was happening in the headlines today? We just announced our earnings." If the job seeker doesn't know that, they appear to be unprepared.

Guide your young job seeker to write out the company mission, research the specific department to which they are applying, and understand what the organization looks like. They should read the company's blog or LinkedIn page. Encourage them to go to Google, enter the firm name, and then click on the "news" tab. Read the top three articles for things that are going on with the company: deals, acquisitions, new hires, etc. This information should ultimately be used to create three bullet points to share what excites them about the company and should be used to answer the questions of, "What do you know about us?" or "Why do you want to work here?" Guide them to review the job description using a highlighter. Highlight the key components of the job and skills requirement, and then compare their skills to the job description. Using this information, they might want to reorder their Skill Stories. For instance, if their skills are analytics, research, and writing and they see that the position is a research heavy role, they'll want to make sure they are ready with their research example first.

This kind of pre-thinking and initial preparation is an important piece of the job search. Even what they're doing the day of an interview in terms of preparing for a video chat—ensuring technology is all working, checking to see that the room they are using is clean—is crucial. An interviewer does not want to see an unmade bed behind a job seeker. They don't want to look at a trashed dorm room. And they don't want to wait while someone tries to get their computer to work.

The biggest mistake that young people make here is not doing any real preparation—or not spending enough time on it—because they're winging it. They think they know enough: "I'll be fine," or, "I know what this company does. This is a parent's friend," or "This is casual. It's just a conversation."

But even if a particular meeting *is* casual, a job seeker looks so much better if they did their homework. Even if the person they are meeting with didn't ask about it, the ability to say, "I was reading the news today and I saw that you just came out with this new product," is a differentiator. Young people know they wing it too much—when I talk about this particular mistake with them, they say it resonates. But even though they see the mistake they're making, they're not sure where to start in terms of fixing it. They need specific instructions on what to do. It's overwhelming and they don't have guidance, so they either do nothing or do too much.

Instead of getting overwhelmed and ignoring this homework altogether, guide your young job seeker to do about an hour of research for each particular role they're interviewing for. It's a matter of gathering and tracking information. Of all the things that you'll ask your young job seeker to do, this piece of the process is probably not going to be as hard as they think it will be. Don't let it eat up an entire week; guide them to do a little research at a time.

Actual employers echo this advice:

"I would highly suggest that as soon as you get an interview with someone, you connect with them on LinkedIn," said Mike Zollenberg, the Chief Clinical Operations Officer at EHE Health. "That means you've at least looked them up and you're trying to figure out who you're talking to. Go to the company's LinkedIn page; watch the webinars, learn about the organization."

Preparation Before a Meeting

Before a meeting, networking call or formal interview, here is how a candidate can use their time wisely to prepare:

- Research the company: Name, CEO, Stock Price (if publicly traded), and write it down.

- Write out the company's overall mission statement as well as the specific department's mission.

- Gain an understanding of the company's organizational structure, business units, key divisions, etc., and know where the department fits into that structure.

- Read the company's blog, LinkedIn page, and/ or Facebook page to get a sense of the tone of the company's content. Or, try reading individual employees' blogs to figure out what type of people work there. Glassdoor.com can also provide a good sense of the company reviews from current and previous employees. (Take them as a guide, not as fact.)

- Search the company's name in the news (i.e., Google "MetLife in the News") to get a sense of anything big going on, any key deals and acquisitions, etc.

- Write down three bullet points about something that excites them about the company.

- Review the job description: using a highlighter, mark key components of the job, skills required, main responsibilities, etc.

- Compare their skills to that of the job description and revise or create two or three Skill Stories to match the requirements.

- Create a side-by-side list comparing what's required versus their skill set.

- Practice speaking about the skills that directly align to the role.

BEFORE THE VIDEO INTERVIEW

If using the video platform for the first time, be familiar with common functions like mute, show video and chat. Also, allow extra time before the meeting starts to download any software.

- Check video and audio before the meeting starts.

- Use a clean, work-appropriate background, select a quiet location, and set the camera at eye level.

- Dress professionally: treat it like an in-person interview as far as dress code.

- Ensure there's good lighting - Turn on lights in the room and/or sit facing the window.

- Remember not to sit in front of a window. Too much light coming from behind makes it difficult to see faces.

- Use earbuds or a headset with a mic for better audio.

SECTION 22:
The Interview... Finally

The most common sentiment from young job seekers is, "If I could only get an interview, I'll be all set."

The good news is that candidates following this process do get interviews. The bad news is they panic about how to prepare for them. You will teach your young job seeker how to prepare for interviews by focusing on their Skill Stories.

This works because any job seeker's three Core Skills serve as the basis for the whole conversation. Be sure the story a candidate has for each of their skills is clear and concise. Two strong stories for each skill is ideal.

Skill Stories serve as the foundation for the majority of anyone's interview answers because *people want to hear stories*. They want to hear about a specific time that the job candidate did something right and solved a problem. So, even if the skill is more generally about how the job seeker worked on the team, they'll need to be able to discuss that from several different angles or by using several different examples: "I had to analyze data as I worked with a team of four. *This* was the role I played. The challenge was *this* and I dealt with it by doing *this*."

"After applications are submitted and they get the interview, communication skills over the phone are very important," said Adrienne Matarazzo, the Talent Acquisition Manager at Veritext. "The candidate must be able to explain why they are an asset to the company. Culture-fit, personality, and skill set are huge. Saying 'eh,' or 'whatever' is a fatal error. Also, I am blown away with the negative stories that candidates share— I've even heard about conflicts they had with someone. They overshare quite a bit.

"We are not only assessing your skills, we are building a culture," Matarazzo continued. "Grads are so scared to speak on the phone. They almost can't even share their skills or communicate effectively."

Prepare Answers Ahead of Time

Your job seeker's aim is this: to make it easy for the interviewer to connect the job seeker's skill to its application. This could involve the candidate repeating themself but interviewers need to understand all the different ways the candidate's skill set could apply to the organization, whether it's how they had to deal with conflicts, how they overcame a challenge, or something similar. To prepare for an interview, the best thing candidates can do is answer a dozen possible interview questions, and practice how they'll incorporate their Skill Stories. While doing so, it's best if they record themselves.

When a young job candidate knows what they want to say, they can direct the conversation toward the example they want to discuss. To help your job seeker, give them a list of possible questions often asked in non-technical interviews and ask them to prepare answers to the five that they think will be really hard for them to answer. A behavioral interview is not technical; it's designed to give a manager a sense of who a new graduate is.

Again, be sure they've done their homework: When Adam Schneider of management consulting firm Oliver Wyman interviews a new college graduate, he is looking for evidence they are interested in this particular role for a career. "If they have not done the homework and do not understand our story—which is readily available on the website—it's a problem. There's no mystery. I don't want to have to explain the job or what my firm does."

DURING THE VIDEO INTERVIEW

Arrive on time or a couple of minutes early

Smile

Look into the camera when speaking, not at the screen

Have a Meeting Plan ready

Eliminate and avoid distractions by not having your phone nearby and by turning off notifications on the computer

Pay attention to the meeting

Sample Interview Questions

The following are typical behavioral interview questions. Pick any five questions that your job seeker would like to focus on first and have them write out answers to these questions. Eventually they will need to prepare for all of them.

1. Tell us how you have demonstrated perseverance or overcome a challenge.

2. Tell me about yourself.

3. Why did you pick your major? How has your education prepared you for your career?

4. What do you know about us? Why did you apply for a role at this company?

5. Tell me how you work in a team.

6. How would your professors/employers describe you? How would your friends describe you?

7. What is your greatest weakness?

8. Where do you see yourself in five years?

9. Share a time you disagreed with a decision that was made by a professor or employer. How did you deal with or resolve this conflict?

10. How will your leadership experiences apply to the work environment? (If applicable.)

11. How would you describe your ideal job?

12. How do you personally define success?

13. What motivates you?

14. What else do you think we should know about you?

15. Why do you think you would be a good fit for this role? Why should we hire you?

16. Why is your GPA not higher?

Once job seekers have answered the questions themselves, the next step is giving them real examples of how others may answer. This is so helpful to the clients we work with as most of them need to be told what to say (at least at first). Because the process can be so overwhelming to first-time job seekers, break it down into little pieces and give your job seeker feedback as they move through each step. Make the process easily consumable.

By reviewing how an expert would answer various interview questions, you're giving young candidates the strategy they need to do well on their own. Guide your new grad to focus on how they have faced a difficult or stressful situation, and how they persisted. Or, how they kept pushing to find an answer in the face of adversity. Invite them to think of a response that showcases how they handled the challenge and also how they might prevent it in the first place.

Even with the simplest questions, remind your job seeker to *listen*. Sometimes, for example, an interviewer might be asking two questions in one. Remind the job seeker to pay attention so they can address both queries. They have to listen to what the interviewer is really asking them. It's okay to ask for clarification: "What is the question, again?" Then, once they understand what the interviewer needs, they have to make a connection between the role and their Core Skills. Guide them to write out answers, practice, and continue to research the company so your job seeker comes across as well informed.

Have your job seeker do mock interviews with peers, family members, or a coach. As they practice, job seekers often realize they can refine their stories and make their skills shine through even better. If they're struggling, encourage interviewees to follow the prompts you've reviewed in this book: "I had a job at XYZ company. I was tasked with putting together *this*. One of the challenges I faced was *this*. And this is how I solved it using this skill." And they have to practice out loud in the mirror, with a parent, with a friend, on video.

Encourage your job seeker to answer interview questions using this framework, because it makes what they are saying easy to follow and it leads to specificity, which interviewers appreciate. They're reminding people where they were, what they were doing, and why it mattered. Keep in mind that the interviewer may not have read their resume ahead of time, so the job seeker will likely have to restate it.

For in-person interviews, be sure to bring a notebook and pen and take notes. When Mike Zollenberg interviews young candidates for roles at EHE Health, he is assessing the following:

- Do they have a good attitude?
- Are they going to do more than what's required?
- Are they prepared?
- Are they trustworthy?

"I can't tell you how many times young people come in and don't even have a notebook," he said. "They're not writing anything down! If you're going to send me a thank you note, why not include some specifics about our conversation? Don't send out the same note to everyone you talk to—and don't misspell names. Show passion. If you're looking to be hired, you should know about the company, who you're talking to, and why you want to be a part of that organization."

JAKE'S STORY

I was very resistant, at first, to get started with Next Great Step. The whole process of trying to find an internship was very anxiety-inducing. I was attempting to do it on my own for a while but realized I didn't know what I was doing and was wasting my time.

In the beginning, I was comparing myself to others even though I didn't know what anyone else was doing. I was thinking, "Why do I need this?" Then, I started to gain confidence in the Next Great Step process after I had my first interview. I used the methods my advisors had shared—and what we had practiced—and felt it went well. The first interview itself was less scary than I thought it was going to be. That was the moment when I relaxed about the whole process.

I'm coming from a history major background and have all of these valuable skills from that—but they're not directly related to any job. My advisor taught me how to focus on tangible outcomes and not fluff in interviews. One of my skills is writing and research, which ended up helping me get an internship doing marketing analytics. I framed it that as a history major, you take straight facts and information and choose how to use them to produce a compelling story.

I have more confidence that I can find the next opportunity and I know how to land the job.

Interview Questions

Here are three examples of questions an interviewer may ask, followed by insight and strong sample answers. Guide your grad to use these as a model to draft their own responses:

Q. Tell us how you have demonstrated perseverance or overcome a challenge.

Here, your job seeker focuses on how they faced a difficult or stressful situation and how they kept persisting to find a solution. Have them demonstrate the ability to keep pushing to find an answer or outcome in the face of adversity. Encourage them to think of an answer that shows their ability to not only handle the challenge, but also to plan ahead to prevent challenges from occurring in the first place. They must show how they take time to dissect and fully understand the problem, plan and prepare for unforeseen challenges, and know when to ask for help.

A. "In a class project, we were assigned to create a new computer program from scratch. The professor created a short deadline on the project. I assessed what was needed and decided what the best approach was based on the budgetary and compliance constraints. Using my analytical skills, I added components systematically one at a time to ensure monitoring of each change. This was difficult and often the computer would not work. I sought guidance from other professors and continued to write and rewrite the code until it was working correctly. Ultimately, the computer program worked and I met the deadline. I am confident in my ability to persevere under challenging constraints and focus on the outcome that exceeded the professor's expectations."

Q. What do you know about us? Why did you apply for a role at this company?

The interviewer wants to know if your job seeker: a) has done their research about the company; b) can describe the company well as an informed outsider; and, c) can translate what they know about the company into expressed interest. Thus, your job seeker must know the employer well enough to be able to describe it in thirty to sixty seconds. Have them look up each company and create a spreadsheet or notes with the name of the CEO, stock price (if applicable), and one to two bullets of current information about the company that is interesting. Have them keep this paper version of the spreadsheet in their portfolio. Remind them to link their Core Skills and experiences as to how they relate to the company. This is also their chance to show how their Core Skills can help the company succeed.

Guide them NOT to answer that it is a good fit for them. It should be about the needs of the organization, not about the needs of your job seeker.

A. "IBM is a global information technology company that sells computer hardware, middleware, and software, and provides hosting and consulting services. Your stock price is showing a turnaround and you are focused on growing your private cloud data platform for enterprise businesses. I applied for a role at your company based on your focus on providing technologies to help businesses and society. I believe my research, communication and leadership skills will help your organization to deliver more artificial intelligence focused products to clients."

"Goldman Sachs is the leading investment bank and provides a wide variety of financial services to corporations, financial institutions, governments, and individuals. Your Institutional Client Services group, where this position is based, works in equity, fixed income, currency, and commodity markets. My internship experience in fixed income, my skills in financial analysis, problem-solving, and analytical skills are well aligned with this role in your fixed income group."

Q. What is your greatest weakness?

The interviewer is exploring three things in this one question: 1) whether the job seeker is self-aware; 2) whether they are honest; and 3) whether they seek to improve. Guide them to keep this answer short and share a weakness that they have been actively working on to improve. They should give an example of what they are doing to overcome this weakness. Every weakness should be turned into a recognized growth opportunity. The interviewer will want to see how the job seeker is dealing with their weaknesses.

Remind them NOT to present their greatest life weakness or something personal. Keep the interview focused on their education and experience.

A. "A weakness for me is that I like to work on something until I feel that it is perfect. What I've realized is that when working in a team or with others, I need to let go and give my piece to the next person so the group can accomplish its goal and meet the deadline. I am aware of this and I have been working to improve it."

"I tend to get caught up in the little details, which can distract me from the ultimate goal. I have overcome this by breaking each project down into mini-tasks, each with their own deadline. If I spend too long on an individual task, I set it aside and move on to the next one. Usually, by the time I come back to the imperfect piece, I can be more objective about whether or not it needs more work."

Young people often get tripped up on the question about weaknesses by being too honest. Remember, this person who is interviewing you is not your doctor or your therapist. Young job seekers go too far and say things like, "I'm just so lazy." No. Remind them to share *a* weakness, not their *greatest* weakness. They should not share something personal like a disability; that's not the interviewer's business. It's all about bringing whatever they say back to the affirmative. Remind them to never speak poorly about other people in their answers.

DAY OF/DURING MEETING TIPS

- Be professionally dressed for in-person meetings
- Arrive 5-10 minutes early

- Bring a portfolio that holds a resume, paper and pen
- Print the Meeting Plan and bring it along; do not use a mobile device
- Shake hands, hold eye contact and smile
- Take notes during the meeting

"I always ask people what they do for fun or what they do outside of work," said Zollenberg. "That's my closing question. I try to get to know them. If they don't have an answer, it shows they can't think on their feet. I ask everyone this question, at every level. In general, what does the candidate who is able to differentiate themselves do in an interview? They share their passion. They've done a lot of research, they have a lot of questions, they've talked to a lot of people. This shows that this candidate is going to come in, figure out what's going on, and be able to help us."

"We need to see flexibility and the ability to be trainable," added Matarazzo. "It's not good if someone is too rigid. After the interview, follow-up is key. They must send a thank you note, say why they are a good fit, and acknowledge what they learned. This sets the candidate apart. Communication is everything. This should be worked on *before* going into an interview. Practice; do mock interviews."

Questions Job Seekers Should Ask

Below is a list of strong questions a young job seeker may ask during any of their interviews, but they must be selected and customized for each interviewer. These should be in the Answers portion of their "3 A's" Meeting Plan. Guide them to pick five to seven questions to memorize.

1. Tell me about your role. What did you do early in your career to help you get here?

2. What are the greatest challenges that you face in this role?

3. How does your company measure its success?

4. What advice would you offer to someone starting out who wants to get into this industry?

5. What are the most significant factors affecting your business today?

6. How has your company grown or changed in the last couple of years?

7. How do you differ from your competition?

8. Describe what it takes for someone to be successful in this company.

9. How do you think most of the employees would describe this workplace?

10. If this company was known for three things as a workplace, what do you think they would be?

SECTION 23:
Follow-Up

For entry-level positions, there is often a second or third interview. Most organizations today are not offering jobs after one interview, and companies are engaging a lot of their employees to help make decisions on a candidate. The guidance for a second or third interview isn't necessarily different than for a first interview, but if there's a person who was in the first interview and in the second as well, the job seeker will need to have to have some additional examples ready to talk about— not just the cookie cutter answer they prepared previously. Make sure that their secondary examples are ready to go, and guide them to look up information about the new person who will be there so they can tailor answers to them.

Encourage your young job seeker to be bold and remember their "3 A's" Meeting Plan. They need to ask the interviewer, "Do you think my skills are aligned with this role? Was there anything that you're seeing that causes you concern?" This is an uncomfortable question for the new graduate to ask, but it's so powerful. Yes, it's bold, but young job seekers have to be more assertive. If they can say, "I'd like to tell you why I am the right fit for this position; I understand your goals. I know I can help you meet them," they will do well.

AFTER A MEETING

Follow up after all interviews with a thank you note. Email and handwritten letters are recommended.

Connect with all of your interviewers on LinkedIn.

Send a follow up every seven days until you receive a status. When following up, send a relevant article or information that adds value.

Thank You Letters

Any follow up to an interview or meeting MUST BE SENT WITHIN 24 HOURS. The job seeker may handwrite or regular mail any letter, but send an email in addition so that it's received promptly. Make sure to personalize all letters for the specific opportunity.

The following are some samples of letters you can customize and send when you are reaching out for a job opportunity, submitting a resume, or following up from a meeting. Refer back to the LinkedIn introduction letters for additional guidance.

THANK YOU LETTER SAMPLE 1:

Dear _____,

Thank you for speaking with me at <u>FAIR/ INTERVIEW</u> I really appreciate it. I would like to reiterate my interest in <u>COMPANY</u>, because of your focus on <u>X</u> and how you do <u>Y</u> in the market. Additionally, I am impressed with <u>COMPANY</u>, because <u>EXAMPLE</u>. I believe that my skills in <u>CORE SKILL THAT CORRELATES WITH JOB</u> and work discipline will go a long way towards <u>COMPANY</u> reaching <u>GOAL</u>. I am confident that I can add value to your organization. I hope you take me into consideration when filling <u>JOB OPPORTUNITY</u>, and thanks again for taking the time to speak to me. I will contact you next week to follow up.

Thanks,

THANK YOU LETTER SAMPLE 2:

Dear _____,

Thank you for the opportunity to interview for the <u>TITLE</u> position in the <u>(PROGRAM OR DEPARTMENT) AT COMPANY</u>. I enjoyed learning more about <u>COMPANY</u> and the many opportunities at the firm, especially in <u>FIELDS OF INTEREST</u>. This really solidified my interest in the company. After understanding the firm's direction, I am confident that I can add value with my experience in <u>SKILLS 1, 2, AND 3</u>. I understand that the goal of <u>COMPANY</u> is to <u>XXX</u> and I can hit the ground running to meet those goals. I am excited about gaining hands-on exposure to a wide range of projects, and developing professionally through <u>COMPANY'S</u> emphasis on training and mentorship. <u>(OR OTHER)</u>.

Once again, I want to thank you for the opportunity to interview for the <u>TITLE</u> position in the <u>(PROGRAM OR DEPARTMENT) AT COMPANY</u>. If you have any further questions about my qualifications, please do not hesitate to call me at <u>PHONE NUMBER</u> or email me at <u>EMAIL</u>. I will call you next week to discuss next steps.

Sincerely,

SHARI RYNAR
HR COORDINATOR, RUTGERS UNIVERSITY

"The landscape has changed in hiring after Covid," Rynar told me in the third quarter of 2021. However, she also noted that a lot hasn't changed. Here is her key advice for new graduates interviewing for their first full-time job:

Show up on time. If you are on time for a 9 a.m. call (walking in or joining a video at 9 a.m.), then in my opinion, you are late. If you show up early, ten minutes before the video or live meeting starts, then you are on time. I want to see that you are waiting ahead of time for the meeting to start.

Ask questions. I like to let the candidate know that the interview is a give and take. You should ask us questions and make sure you are clear about the role. Too often, the candidate is not listening and expands on a question that was not asked.

Appearance is important. Don't chew gum or eat during the interview. Put your phone away and shut off all notifications. Dress professionally. Put up a background that is not distracting for virtual interviews. If you have to take the call from Starbucks due to Wi-Fi or other issues, state that up front.

Turn off your own image on the screen so you don't look at yourself. You should be looking at me or at the camera directly. Finally, you will need good lighting—I want to be able to see you.

Things that Rynar wishes job seekers knew:

Don't randomly apply if the skills you have do not meet the requirements.

Their strengths: soft skills are way more important than hard skills. If someone can look me in the eye and communicate well, they can be taught the other skills of the job.

They need to sell themselves. Boast about your strengths. Don't start defending your faults when no one asks about that.

Less is more: Stick to what is being asked and put a hard stop on your answer. Only answer the questions that are asked.

"Get everyone's name, email and phone number on the search committee. Call back. Also ask, 'When can I expect to hear back. What does my future look like?' The interview does?not end—it continues until the candidate is chosen. Finally, you must send a thank you note. Sadly, only 60% of candidates send a note. Look up the correct spelling of every name. My favorite saying is 'Measure twice. Cut once.'"

When They Are Rejected

Rejection happens, and it's hard. Not every interview series results in a job offer or internship, so the question is, how should a young job seeker follow up? When someone says *thank you but no thank you*, it's okay for the job seeker to ask for another meeting or call to understand why they didn't get the job. If the job seeker really wants to be successful, understanding what they will need to do as a candidate is crucial.

This conversation becomes another "3 A's" Meeting Plan. Guide your new graduate to take a very humble approach, as in, "I'm really excited about your company and would love to understand what I need to do to better position myself for a future opportunity, whether it's training or shadowing. What kind of experiences do you want to see from me?"

Companies love this because the job seeker is showing initiative and emphasizing they are self-aware.

I worked with a candidate recently who was devastated to not receive an offer after a third interview round. When it comes down to your job seeker and one other person after the third or fourth interview, it's okay for them to ask for feedback. This particular candidate asked the hiring manager why they made the decision that they did. The manager said, "We were really impressed with you—it's just that this other person had a few more years of experience. But because we truly are so impressed you came back to us to ask for more information, when the next opening comes up, you're going to be the first person we call."

She would not have known that without making the call. Furthermore, I don't know whether the organization would have given her that second shot if she hadn't initiated the conversation. There's so much rejection when young people are looking for a job and it's easy for them to withdraw. I'll ask our young clients what happened when they did not progress with a promising opportunity, and all they will say is, "I don't know." You're never going to know and you're not going to learn if you don't ask for feedback.

CHAPTER SEVEN KEY TAKEAWAYS

- Everybody thinks that if they just fix their resume, they will be fine. This kind of thinking is a huge mistake because it's just not true.

- A resume needs to be clear, concise, and easy to read. It's all about how they can make this process as painless as possible for the person who has to evaluate them.

- The biggest mistake that young people make is not doing any real preparation for an interview, or not spending enough time on it.

- Skill Stories serve as the foundation for the majority of anyone's interview answers because people want to hear stories.

- Your job seeker's aim is this: to make it easy for the interviewer to connect the job seeker's skill to its application in their company.

Ace the Virtual Interview

Virtual Interviews are the new way of the world. Is your job seeker prepared? Do they know how to prepare differently for a virtual interview compared to in-person interviews? This checklist provides key tips to ace the virtual interview before, during and after.

nextgreatstep.com/bookresources

WHERE DO WE GO FROM HERE?

I know the tone of the book has been very "can do," and that was intentional because your student or new grad absolutely can do what it takes to land their first job. But it might not happen immediately or in the manner they pictured it happening. The truth is every single human being launching a career deals with setbacks, false starts, and frustrating near-misses. Often, these setbacks have nothing to do with the job seeker, what they said or didn't say, or what they did or didn't do.

Sometimes a setback is just a random thing, and they happen to everyone. A job offer is rescinded. A company files for bankruptcy. A contract is canceled or scaled back. One of my favorite phrases is, "Please pardon my persistence," because persistence is the not-so-secret sauce of any successful career.

The last thing you want is for your young job seeker to settle into despair after one or two rejections, because the best careers are often built on a pile of hundreds of "no's."

Careers are not going to fall into place. It's not going to be exactly how they want or what they thought it was going to be. They may hate their first boss and need to find a different position after a short time. Thus, the ability to persevere is everything.

Two million bachelor's degrees are awarded in the United States to new graduates each year and over nineteen million students are currently enrolled in degree-granting post-secondary colleges. These students face bracing statistics:

- The unemployment rate for young adults is regularly as high as 25% and over 40% of recent graduates report being underemployed.

- Only 30% of grads have the skills needed to be successful in the market but most feel unprepared to get a job.

- 30-40% have diagnosable anxiety.

- Four out of ten students never use Career Services at their colleges or universities.

- While 87% of new grads say they are well prepared, only 50% of managers agree.

My heart goes out to parents who say, "I put my son through the program and I've given him every resource. He is doing everything right yet still experiences rejection."

THE NEXT GREAT STEP

Results

Fortunately, when we guide new graduates to use the process you just read about, they see results. **Ninety percent of our clients are landing the jobs they desire within 3-5 months of applying this approach**. They go from feeling confused, lost and in limbo, to feeling confident and purposeful.

I share our approach to empower parents and others to guide their own students and grads in a strategic and simplified manner so they can help in the right way—a proven methodology that works. From one parent to another, let me tell you that this process takes time.

The key is patience and persistence.

After learning the steps in this process, your student or young job seeker will start to feel more confident. They will know what they're saying in meetings. You'll overhear them in an interview and understand that they're at a totally different level from where they started. As one father recently said of his daughter before engaging her in the program, "She needs directions with a structured approach. Doing it consistently with the support of a coach, not just a doting father, will make all the difference. Hearing from an expert that she should consider a different way will really help her. This training will benefit my daughter for the rest of her life, because she'll learn to say what she wants and what she is able to offer by putting this process into practice. This is the missing piece. She has to define success for herself and run with that." He sees that his daughter has great value but has not been able to articulate (to herself) what she is seeking from a professional job. Thus, he believed our program would be able to help her.

Even more significant than this initial win, however, is the lifetime value of a young person understanding how to define and articulate their contributions and skill set in professional settings. This ability—and the confidence that comes from developing it—will help them not only secure their first full-time job offer, it will pay dividends when it's time for your child to ask for a raise or promotion, or pursue a new opportunity at a different organization years down the road.

By giving your student or graduate a clear framework for job seeking with unambiguous steps, their anxiety will lessen and their confidence will grow. Next Great Step has a proven track record of success and is solely focused on helping clients nineteen to twenty-nine years old with their job search. We designed our services to speak directly to parents, students and new college graduates launching into their first internships or full-time jobs. With proven business experience, we understand what companies and organizations expect of students or recent graduates and know that 80% of jobs are found by referral—*not* by randomly applying to online postings.

Our expertise, data, and insights have been featured in *CNN*, *Fortune*, *Kiplinger*, *The New York Times* and *The Wall Street Journal*. We've appeared on SiriusXM with the Wharton School as well as CNBC and several national TV news segments. I serve as a frequent guest on several Apple and Spotify podcasts. The most common question we are asked is, "What is your measure of success for a student who goes through the program? How do I know they will really do this?" I tell parents that it does not matter how much they or I think this program will be beneficial for their child. Their student or graduate has to really want it. They need to have experienced enough difficulty in trying to accomplish something on their own. When they are ready to try a new way of thinking and to commit to the process, we know they will see success.

As a parent, I know this is easier said than done. That's why my team and I at Next Great Step would be honored to support you and your grad. We understand as experts—and parents— how difficult this process can be. We've found that one of the most powerful aspects of the service we offer is not just the coaching and process framework we provide but in the camaraderie our young clients develop with one another. It is a huge comfort to young graduates who have not yet secured a job offer to meet others just like them who are struggling in the exact same way. This problem is very common.

You are not alone, and they are not alone. Each year, thousands of students and new college graduates embark on the process of finding a job or internship. There is no reason to do it without support. It takes a village, and we are here to cheer you on through this process.

Please accept our sincere appreciation for reading this book. We wish you and your grad good luck, but remember, luck arrives when preparation meets opportunity!

ACKNOWLEDGMENTS

When I launched this business, I had no idea of the scale of this problem. I had been in the consulting world and saw the desire companies had to hire young talent. I also saw, however, that they kept passing on new college graduates for a multitude of reasons. My friends' kids went to great schools yet could not land that first full-time job offer.

The Next Great Step approach was born. It started as the strategic planning process I facilitated with my father to help CEOs and their executive teams compete globally. Only when Peter Blacksberg, our dear family friend, made us aware of this gap between college students and employers did we see how our strategy could be at the forefront of solving the career path issue for young adults. He knew preparing students and new grads for their first full-time job search was not happening at scale. Peter helped prove we were all seeing an urgent problem that needed to be solved. I am thankful for his vision that led me to this path.

My father Harvey Hendler is the inventor of many of the Next Great Step concepts. He taught this methodology to countless corporate clients after developing its roots in the strategic planning and consulting he did for C-suites around the globe. His input has made the Next Great Step approach possible and extremely effective. More importantly, he has always been my most devoted mentor and advisor on all aspects of my professional career. His belief and confidence in my abilities has enabled me to achieve the success our company enjoys today. I constantly seek his advice and input. I am so lucky to have him in my life.

I'd also like to thank my family for supporting me, trusting me, and being willing to serve as the guinea pigs for this process. When I started this business, my sons were 13 and 16 years old. They had no idea what was in store for them. Fortunately, when I made the leap from gainfully employed consultant to round-the-clock entrepreneur, my husband Jeff Grunt was my biggest supporter. Although there may have been times he questioned the hours and the effort I was putting into this business, he has been an incredible advisor, confidante and cheerleader. His experience as founder of his own small business has been of immeasurable value to me in terms of the advice and insight he offers. I am so appreciative of his love and support.

Next, I'd like to extend my gratitude to my eldest son Brandon Grunt. As a recent grad, he was the test case for much of my work. Brandon went through his four years of college as I was developing this business. He listened (not always willingly at first!) and followed my advice to network and build relationships. I'm so pleased to be able to announce that his efforts paid off with four internships that enabled him to successfully launch his career. Thank you also to my younger son Jacob Grunt, a current college student who has heard me give my pitch so many times he knows it by heart. He's next to get schooled on the NGS process!

When I graduated from Washington University in St. Louis, I left with a wonderful education and lifelong friends. I had no idea that my college roommate would be such an instrumental part of this business. Thank you to Lauren Aaron, our VP. As my college roomie, right and left hand, and best friend, she has consistently told me the hard truth when no one else would. I am eternally grateful to her. Likewise, she will do anything to support, grow, and protect our business. I could not do any of it without her. I also want to thank Rachel Scherzer, the senior advisor to our NGS clients. She has such a warm and empathetic way with our young job seekers, ensuring they consistently achieve success. The first person I entrusted to teach this process, Rachel has consistently and completely exceeded my expectations.

Next, I'd like to recognize several key advisors in the NGS ecosystem. Thank you to Steve Fleischer, one of my first parent clients and biggest supporters of our mission. He has become a key advisor and was instrumental in giving feedback on the voice of the parent as I wrote this book. I am so grateful to Steve for continually validating the importance of this effort. I'd also like to thank Tim Barton, my own coach, who provided support and guidance every step of the way. Tim always has me consider new ideas and pushes me to try new things. I'd like to thank Dr. Dawn Graham as well. After I sent her a cold letter pitching myself to be on her SiriusXM radio show, Dr. Graham became a close colleague who shares the same passion and mission as NGS to help young adults achieve career success. For her guidance, advice, and support in writing this book's foreword, I am grateful. Thank you also to Harris Nydick, my financial advisor and fellow author who gave so much of his time and effort to advise and provide feedback on the book.

I'd like to recognize my village of friends and colleagues who advised me during the writing process, collaborated with me on some of the book's ideas, or were willing to be quoted. Incredibly successful in each of their respective industries, I am lucky to call Nancy Josephs, Shari Rynar, Mike Zollenberg, and Amy Schwartz close friends. I am so thankful for my professional relationships with Joe Battista, Julia Turovsky, Dave Peterschmidt, Elizabeth Kostolansky, Adrienne Matarazzo, and Adam Schneider who gave of their time to advise and collaborate on this effort. Thank you.

Finally, I'd like to thank Amber Vilhauer and her marketing team, and Laura Schaefer and Ashley Bunting, the professionals who helped me with book writing and publishing.

ABOUT
THE AUTHOR

Beth Hendler-Grunt is the founder and president of Next Great Step. She is a dynamic leader, advisor, and facilitator who has extensive experience consulting to startups, Fortune 500 firms, universities, and individuals. The sole focus of Next Great Step is to guide students and recent grads to help them to achieve career success. Ms. Hendler-Grunt leverages techniques and insights of guiding CEOs and brings those secrets to students to help them stand out and get the job. Ms. Hendler-Grunt and her team have helped hundreds of college students and grads launch their careers via one-on-one coaching, group sessions, and public speaking engagements for individuals and schools. She has been featured in the *Wall Street Journal, The New York Times, CNN, Fortune, Kiplinger,* SiriusXM Radio, CNBC and many other media outlets. Her clients have landed jobs at Amazon, JP Morgan, Fox News, and ESPN to name a few.